Bright Flowers

TEXTILES AND CERAMICS OF CENTRAL ASIA

Christina Sumner and Guy Petherbridge

ph^m **powerhouse publishing**
part of the Powerhouse Museum

in association with

LUND HUMPHRIES

Frontispiece and detail above: **Suzani** (wall hanging). There is little difference between field and border in this suzani, each rosette is unique and the background is filled with flowers, leaves and scattered kitchen knife motifs.

● Silk *yurma* (tamboured chain stitch) on *karbos* (hand-woven cotton), *zeh* (woven edging) border with *popuk* (tassels), made in Shafirkhan near Bukhara, Uzbekistan, late 1800s.

295 x 157 cm

Opposite: **Storage jar** (*khum*). The vertical design of these jars permits efficient use of storage space and allows for transport by camel, horse and donkey.

● Lead-glazed earthenware, built from wheel-thrown components, exterior and interior monochrome green glazed, gas-kiln fired, made by Usto Rajab Ortiqov, Khiva, Khorezm region, Uzbekistan, 2002. 65 x 35.6 cm

See page 152

Previous page: Detail of bowl excavated in the Isfara district, Sogd region, Tajikistan, late 1100s–early 1200s.
See page 118

READERS NOTE: THIS PUBLICATION USES THE BEFORE THE COMMON ERA (BCE)/ COMMON ERA (CE) DATING SYSTEM.

MEASUREMENTS ARE CENTIMETRES (CM), HEIGHT X WIDTH/DIAMETER/ LENGTH X DEPTH

First published in 2004 by
Powerhouse Publishing, Sydney
PO Box K346 Haymarket NSW 1238
Australia
in association with
Lund Humphries
Gower House
Croft Road, Aldershot
Hampshire GU11 3HR
United Kingdom

Powerhouse Publishing is part of the Museum of Applied Arts and Sciences
www.powerhousemuseum.com/publish
Lund Humphries is part of Ashgate Publishing
www.lundhumphries.com

National Library of Australia CIP (pb)
Sumner, Christina.
Bright flowers: textiles and ceramics of Central Asia.
Bibliography. Includes index.
ISBN 1 86317 106 1 (pbk)
1. Powerhouse Museum - Exhibitions. 2. Art, Central Asian - Exhibitions.
I. Petherbridge, Guy, 1944- . II.Powerhouse Museum. III. Title.
709.580749441

British Library Cataloguing-in-Publication Data (hc)
A catalogue record for this book is available from the British Library
ISBN 0 85331 912 X (hc)
Library of Congress Control Number: 2004111170

Editing: Colette Batha
Design: Peter Thorn Design
Project management: Julie Donaldson
Scanning: Ryan Hernandez & Spitting Image
Prepress: Spitting Image
Printing: Produced through Phoenix Offset, printed in China

Published in conjunction with the exhibition *Bright flowers: textiles and ceramics of Central Asia* at the Powerhouse Museum September 2004 – February 2005 Developed by the Powerhouse Museum from the state collections of Uzbekistan, Tajikistan and Kazakhstan and private collections of Guy Petherbridge and Dee Court. Supported by UNESCO, AusHeritage, Heritage Central Asia, National Commissions for UNESCO in Uzbekistan, Tajikistan and Kazakhstan, Gordon Darling Foundation and Oriental Rug Society (NSW).

Distributed by Lund Humphries/Ashgate in all territories outside Australia and New Zealand (hard cover only)
Distributed in Australia and New Zealand by Bookwise International.

Contents

Central Asia

Aral
Sea

KAZAKHSTAN

ALMATY →

④ • Otrar

Taraz •

UZBEKISTAN

KARAKALPAKSTAN

• Shimkent

BISHKEK

Syr Darya

• Kunya Urgench

• Nukus

KYRGYZSTAN

Urgench
Khorezm

Khiva • Khanki
Kattabag

② ☆ **TASHKENT**

Ferghana Valley

• Namangan

• Nurata

Gurumsaray •
Andijon •

Gizduvan •

• Shafirkhan

Margilan •

TURKMENISTAN

• Vabkent
(Uba)

Jizzak •

Rishtan •

Kanibadam •

Ferghana

• **BUKHARA**

Kattakurgan •

Isfara •
Chorku •

• Kattakurgan

Khudjand •

KASHGAR

Ashgabat

① **SAMARKAND** ☆

• Ura Tube

(Afrasiab) ⑤ • Urgut

TAJIKISTAN

IRAN

• Kitab
• Kasan Shakhrisabz

③

Merv

Kasbi •
Kashkadarya

☆ **DUSHANBE**

BADAKHSHAN

Nishapur •
Mashad

Amu Darya

• Boysun

Khatlon

Pamirs

Sukhandarya

Denau •

Khulbok •

Termez

Faisabad •

AFGHANISTAN

Herat •

Archaeological sites
① Afrasiab
② Chorsu
③ Merv
④ Otrar
⑤ Ulugbek Madrasa

Traditional
Silk Road trade routes

Left: A market stall in
Karakalpakstan.

PHOTO BY CHRISTINA SUMNER, 2003

Forewords

Bright flowers: textiles and ceramics of Central Asia has been published in association with an international loan exhibition of the same name which brings to Australian audiences unique and beautiful urban embroideries and glazed ceramics from the state museum collections of Central Asia. It is a rare occurrence for such treasures to leave the region and this is the first time they have come to Australia. The Powerhouse Museum welcomes this opportunity for cultural cooperation with Central Asian museum colleagues and the governments of Uzbekistan, Tajikistan and Kazakhstan. These relationships create new possibilities for cultural exchange and further support the Powerhouse's activities in the Asian region.

The Powerhouse Museum's engagement with Central Asia began in 1885, soon after the Museum was founded, when a folio of fifty chromolithographs depicting Central Asian ornamentation was acquired in London for the Museum's embryonic collection. The Museum now holds Australia's largest collection of international and Australian decorative arts and design, including significant Asian holdings which reflect the Museum's ongoing commitment to programs that foster a greater understanding of the richness and diversity of Asian cultures. The value of the Museum's collection as a resource for students, collectors and specialists, as well as general visitors, is greatly enhanced by the display of related material from collections in the region.

The *Bright flowers* exhibition and this publication are the result of several years of research, negotiation and visits to the region by Powerhouse Museum curator Christina Sumner and Guy Petherbridge, chairman Heritage Central Asia, whose involvement in the region and expertise in Central Asian ceramics have been invaluable.

Dr Kevin Fewster
DIRECTOR, POWERHOUSE MUSEUM

We welcome the organisation by the Powerhouse Museum of the exhibition *Bright flowers: textiles and ceramics of Central Asia*, which is drawn in part from the National Museums of Ethnography and Archaeology of Tajikistan. Other lenders are the state museums of Bukhara, Samarkand and Tashkent in Uzbekistan, Nukus in Karakalpakstan and Almaty in Kazakhstan. This publication, which accompanies the exhibition, offers valuable insights into the history of material culture throughout these ancient Central Asian nations.

The origin of textile and ceramic production and ornamentation in the region dates back many centuries. Written and archaeological sources show that many of the decorative patterns can be traced to the Persian ancestors of the Tajiks of today; other designs reflect the nomadic antecedents of the Uzbek, Kazakh and Karakalpak peoples. A wide range of handcrafted artifacts such as dowry textiles, costume and accessories, storage jars, bowls, cups and jugs were produced and richly decorated by the most skilled craftswomen and men.

Today we in Tajikistan are happily experiencing a resurgence in the demand for traditional arts and crafts, especially from visitors to the region, as is also occurring elsewhere in Central Asia. Creativity and artistry in the production of traditional crafts is very much alive today and reflects the antiquity of the parent cultures. We welcome the exhibition and this publication which communicate to a wide audience the unique and beautiful embroidered textiles and glazed ceramics of Central Asia.

Professor Rakhim Masov
DIRECTOR, INSTITUTE OF HISTORY, ARCHAEOLOGY AND ETHNOGRAPHY
ACADEMY OF SCIENCES OF THE REPUBLIC OF TAJIKISTAN

Introduction

Christina Sumner

An hour after first arriving in ancient Bukhara in central Uzbekistan, I sat beside the Labi-hauz pool, gazing at the gnarled old mulberry trees reflected in the still waters of the pond. The peaceful seventeenth-century Labi-hauz plaza is a favourite meeting place in Bukhara, where generations of men have gathered to drink tea and play chess and where international visitors now come to pass the time of day.

On the east side of the Labi-hauz stands the Nadir Divanbegi Madrasa, originally built as a *caravanserai*, its façade bright with turquoise, cobalt and white tiles; to the south are the remains of the city's old Jewish quarter. I watched as my Tajik guide poured tea into a small porcelain bowl and emptied it back into the pot. She did this three times. '*Loi, moi, choi*. The first time it's mud, the second oil, and the third tea' she explained, 'and always pour the first cup for yourself and the second for your guest to show it's not poisoned'. Her words echoed the sacred hospitality so graciously observed by the Central Asians, whose generosity and kindness have warmed my sojourns there. It was also a startling reminder of a dangerous past. This is a region of dramatic and robust history with its conquests, catastrophes and shifting power bases.

Opposite: suzani detail
(see page 65)

The 16th-century Taqi-Telpak Furushon, once a bazaar and now a craft market, with the Kalon Minaret behind. Bukhara, central Uzbekistan.
PHOTO BY CHRISTINA SUMNER, 1999

I had travelled to Central Asia on a research visit for Sydney's Powerhouse Museum, with a view to establishing new museum-sector relationships for Australia in the Asian region and evaluating options for collaborative projects. I had come, like thousands before me, primed with dreams and legendary tales, and full of curiosity. Not well-known to the outside world, landlocked Central Asia was once the heartland of the Silk Road trading network. It is an extraordinarily diverse region geographically, with an interesting ethnic mix, a long-term symbiotic relationship between settled and nomadic modes of subsistence and rich decorative traditions. Like many of those earlier travellers also, I had come with a mission. I wanted to see the state museums and their collections, and in particular to view their holdings of traditional urban embroidered textiles.

The courtyard and tiled entrance to Tashkent's Museum of Applied Arts, built for a wealthy Tsarist diplomat by craftsmen from Bukhara, Samarkand, Tashkent and Ferghana.

PHOTO BY CHRISTINA SUMNER, 1999

Elsewhere in the region my colleague Guy Petherbridge, Director of Australia's AusHeritage organisation, was on a parallel quest, pursuing his deep interest in the region's glazed ceramic traditions, as well as developing for UNESCO a cultural heritage management blueprint for Central Asia. Our shared vision was to curate an exhibition of textiles and ceramics from the state museum collections of the region for display in Australia. This publication, and the exhibition it records, are the collective realisation of that intention. Our shared hope is that, through this opportunity for close encounters with these bright and truly splendid textiles and ceramics, Australians and others will come to appreciate and more fully understand the cultures that gave rise to them.

Throughout the project, one of the most stimulating challenges has been to try and build mind bridges between traditional past and contemporary reality, to identify and document transformations in the design and production of objects over time. In Central Asia, seeking to understand and interpret the material culture must include many historical factors: the seductive romanticism of the Silk Road, with its camel trains winding through deserts and high passes, exotic trade goods, markets, courts and fabled *caravanserais*; the coming of Islam with Muslim armies from the west in the eighth century; Mongol incursions from the north-east in the 1200s; the conquests and subsequent architectural and artistic achievements of the Timurid era in the 1300s; the elimination of slavery, increased freedom for women and the rise of collectivisation in the Tsarist Russian and Soviet eras; and the post-independence modernity and patriotism of those living in the Central Asian republics today.

Although the embroidered textiles and dress illustrated in this publication were produced during the last 150 years or so (very few earlier examples have survived), their design and imagery demonstrate multicultural influences which date back many centuries. Ceramics of course have much greater durability, and we are therefore able to include pots that date back to Timurid and earlier tenth-century Samanid times, when the Silk Road trade was flourishing.

About the region

Often simply referred to as Central Asia, western Central Asia today consists of the five independent states of Kazakhstan, Kyrgyzstan, Tajikistan, Turkmenistan and Uzbekistan. Until its dissolution in 1991, these states, established along cultural/linguistic lines during the Soviet era, were previously part of the Soviet Union. Whilst under Tsarist rule in the 1800s, the region was known as Russian Turkestan or western Turkestan. The people of the region then consisted of nomadic groups around the oasis cities of Khiva and Kokand and Bukhara which were largely inhabited by Uzbeks (rulers), Turkmen (military), and Tajiks (bureaucrats, artisans and farmers). Eastern Turkestan, or eastern Central Asia, is now the autonomous Chinese province of Xinjiang. Geographically, much of Central Asia consists of a great expanse of arid grassland (steppe), desert and semi-desert stretching from central Europe in the west to the Pacific coast of Siberia in the east. Mountain chains, notably the Tien Shan (Celestial Mountains) which reach from Xinjiang to Kyrgyzstan and the high Pamirs that extend across Tajikistan, are flung westwards from the Mongolian Altai and the Tibetan Himalayas, dividing and protecting the plains.

In the foothills of the mountains where streams abound, and in the river valley oases, the land is green and fertile, offering an ideal environment for settled living based economically on agriculture. In the steppes to the north and semi-desert to the west and east, nomadic groups traditionally followed a pastoral way of life. The people practising these two modes of subsistence have always been strongly interconnected, the boundaries between them porous and negotiable; indeed, at the junction of the two ecological zones, the same people engaged in both agriculture and pastoralism. These different subsistence modes broadly determined the people's material culture. It is possible to say, albeit simplistically, that while nomad women characteristically wove rugs and tent bags with wool from their animals, settled women typically embroidered large wall hangings of silk and cotton, fibres which are dependent on the cultivation of plants. While handbuilt pots with incised, moulded or painted decoration can be made anywhere and fired in the campfire, wheel-made glazed ceramics require a more permanent location for a studio and a kiln.

Central Asia has always been a unique cultural ecology where three very different ways of life intersect. To pastoral nomadism and irrigation agriculture must be added a thousand years of cross-cultural Silk Road trade, which involved herder and farmer alike in commodity trading and provisioning the caravans. This continual traffic exposed the people of the region to an exceptional range of social, religious, scientific, aesthetic and ideological influences, primarily from Iran, India, China and, from the 1700s onwards, Russia. Despite the general wholesale shift from overland to sea trade in the 1500s, the traditional routes to India via Afghanistan, China via Xinjiang and Europe via Iran stayed open and trade remained a significant factor in Central Asian life.

A young Tajik girl picking flowers near the ruins of the Ak-Saray, Amir Timur's (Tamerlane's) summer palace, in Shakhrisabz. Kashkadaryia province, Uzbekistan.
PHOTO BY CHRISTINA SUMNER, 2003

People, language and nationhood

The characteristically carved and painted walls of the *ivan* (covered terrace) in the inner courtyard of the Fayzulla Khujaev House in Bukhara, now part of the State Museum complex. Central Uzbekistan.

PHOTO BY CHRISTINA SUMNER, 2002

The earliest inhabitants of the region were Indo-Iranians who spoke a language closely related to Farsi and are the ancestors of today's Tajiks, who still speak a dialect of Farsi. They settled in the foothills and oases of Central Asia in the late Neolithic period and created a distinctive lifestyle based on irrigation agriculture and long distance trade. The Kazakhs, Kyrgyz, Turkmen and Uzbeks all speak Turkic languages, one of the lasting legacies of the incoming waves of nomadic Turks who, competing for lands and power, came from the far north-east from the sixth century. The last of these groups, the Uzbeks, arrived on the scene in the 1400s.

The use of different languages over the long-term in Central Asia has given rise to inconsistencies and confusion regarding terminology in the textile field. Having different words for a man's robe in different languages (*chapan* in Uzbek, *khalat* in Russian and *joma* in Tajik) is only to be expected. With time, the movement of people and the separation of communities, people who speak the same language may adopt different terms for the same object, or the same term for different objects, in different parts of the country. The Tajik embroidery term *kanda khayol* has been described to me variously by local specialists as meaning the lively spotted effect of chain stitch worked in two alternating colours and a form of couching stitch. Hence, there is likely to be disagreement with our use and assigned meanings of some terms in this publication; for all such infelicities we apologise in advance and accept full responsibility.

The increasing focus on nationalism in the five Western Central Asian states following their independence from the Soviet Union in the early 1990s has fostered a strong sense of identity among people of different ethnic origins, but it has also brought about much separation. The origin of this separation can be found in Soviet policy which deliberately increased dialectic differences and enforced the ethnic separation that resulted in the formation of the five states. Russian was the *lingua franca* of the Soviet Union, taught in schools and understood by most. Today, learning Russian has been largely discontinued in favour of English, the international language of diplomacy. Where once travel between the different states was easy, interstate travel is becoming more problematic. A special permit is now required to drive the direct route from Tashkent to Samarkand, as the road crosses a projecting piece of Kazakhstan.

Embracing statehood and nationalism has however strongly encouraged the production, and in some instances revival, of the spectacularly beautiful and varied traditional arts and crafts of the region. The origins of these works, created by women and men from both classic urban and nomadic modes of existence, can be found well in the past.

Islamic and other influences

Prior to the spread of Islam into Central Asia in the eighth century, artists and artisans were not limited in their choice of subject matter for the decoration of their walls, textiles, costumes, jewellery and everyday objects of wood, metal and clay. Patterns and motifs reflected ancient and deeply embedded animist and shamanist beliefs and traditions from the nomad world, as well as the long-term cross-cultural aesthetic influences of Persia, Europe, China and India, and the religious influences of Buddhism and Zoroastrianism. Under Islam decoration became predominantly geometric and ornamental, composed of stylised plants and geometric patterns.

From a design perspective, the strongest artistic influence came from Iran and the floral patterns and motifs so prevalent in the works of Iranian artists inspired their Central Asian counterparts, the potters, embroiderers and other craftspeople. Gloriously decorative architectural ornament such as wood carving, *ganch* (plaster carving) and wall painting, as well as metalwork, ceramics, carpets and embroidery, all featured gracefully stylised trees, leafy tendrils and flowers, flowers and more flowers. Artists and artisans filled the available surfaces with pattern and colour, creating interiors, costume and artefacts whose brilliance contrasted flamboyantly with the blank exterior walls of the houses and the starkness of the surrounding unwatered landscape. In modern Central Asia, this contrast between exterior and interior is still striking, a legacy perhaps of the human imperative to create personal safety and beauty in the sanctuary of family and home within the external realities of nomadic incursions, famine, poverty, oppression, and the surrounding desiccating desert.

Because women in both urban and rural societies have been characteristically embedded in the continuum of popular beliefs and local customs related to hearth and home, they tend to observe the more formal face of Islam less assiduously than men. This is reflected in the spontaneity, variety and freedom of expression found in women's domestic arts, compared with the craft output of men for the public domain, such as the decoration of mosques, madrasas and mausolea. This is not to say that women did not or do not observe Islam; in devout Margilan in the Ferghana Valley I was invited to attend a women-only feast to celebrate the commitment to memory by my hostess of the entire Koran.

A Central Asian miniature showing a section of the bazaar where textiles and ceramics were sold side by side. On the left are shelves stacked with printed or embroidered textiles and fine robes; among the vessels on the right are blue-and-white lidded jars which were probably produced locally by potters inspired by Chinese designs.
PLATE 199 FROM *MINIATURES ILLUSTRATIONS OF ALISHER NAVOI'S WORKS OF THE 15TH-19TH CENTURIES*, UZBEK SSR ACADEMY OF SCIENCES, 1982

Decline, survival, revival

The diaries of early travellers to the region and reports by Russian scholars are indispensible to Central Asian material culture studies. As Soviet scholarship becomes increasingly accessible to western researchers, we can look forward to a progressively greater understanding of this fabulous body of traditional arts.

The decline of traditional domestic crafts began under Tsarist rule in Turkestan in the latter half of the 1800s. Women's labour was required in the economically vital cotton fields, resulting in less time at home. After the Bolshevik Revolution in 1917, Soviet policy set out to transform traditional craft workers into workers for the state. Existing craft guilds were reformed as professional unions and the craft workers themselves gradually came together, first into ateliers and workshop cooperatives and then, with the introduction of modern machinery, into factories.

Although skills such as wood and *ganch* carving, brass work, leatherwork, embroidery and weaving, practised in the oasis towns and villages have been retained and even encouraged, the survival of others was threatened by factory-made goods. Craft-based pottery in particular has suffered from the introduction of aluminium, enamel and factory-made chinaware. Textile consumption profiles changed as materials and products, for example silks and velvets which were previously only affordable to the wealthy, became more generally available. The legacy can still be seen in Central Asia today in the bright, floral-patterned factory-made velvets and synthetics preferred by the many women who still wear traditional Central Asian dress of trousers, long overdress and headscarf.

A predilection for familiar, traditional furnishings and decoration in domestic interiors supported some aspects of

An Uzbek textile trader, inheritor of an ancient tradition, at the Urgut Sunday market. The women are wearing traditional Central Asian dress. Near Samarkand, central Uzbekistan.
PHOTO BY CHRISTINA SUMNER, 1999

production. Floors were still covered with nomadic- or village-made felted or flat-woven rugs, but the suzanis of the Soviet era were generally no match for the exquisite stitching of nineteenth-century Tajik or Uzbek women and girls for their dowry chests. Although Central Asian women continued to make traditional decorative objects, with some adaptations to style or technique, for their own domestic use and for sale to others through unofficial channels, characteristic of the period are the suzanis produced by men working in factories with chain-stitch sewing machines on factory-woven cloth.

Today the traditional style of interior decoration endures, especially in rural areas. Living is comfortable with piles of brightly coloured quilts and cushions set around a low table; during the day the sleeping quilts are stacked on top of the dowry chest and covered with a *nim* (half-size) suzani. In many homes these are augmented by western-style tables and chairs, glossy glass-fronted cabinets and machine-woven carpets as wall hangings. In Tashkent, the preferred dowry items now tend more towards furniture, china and glassware than traditional suzanis; in Bukhara however a girl must still have four suzanis set aside for her wedding day.

The corpus of Central Asian traditional crafts today, in relation to design, materials and artisanship, varies greatly as contemporary artists, potters, metalworkers, miniaturists and embroiderers grapple with the familiar twenty-first century economic dilemma of the relationship between time, productivity, quality and demand. The establishment by UNESCO of subsidised carpet-weaving workshops in Bukhara and Khiva enables the weavers to produce old designs anew with the finest naturally dyed yarns. In the Abdul Khasim Madrasa craft collective in Tashkent, miniaturists work their exquisite gilded enchantment on lacquer boxes and wood carvers magically extract complex folding Koran stands from single pieces of wood. Suzani makers are multiplying rapidly in the Bukhara region, although only a few can replicate the extraordinarily fine needlework of their grandmothers and earlier generations. In Shakhrisabz, the traditional local craft of *iroqi*, a form of needlepoint, is enjoying a high-quality, high-profile revival in the hands of dedicated entrepreneurs, in forms designed to suit both local and tourist markets. Although the living ceramic tradition of making brilliantly coloured glazed wares is in danger of extinction after some 1200 years of continuity, joint initiatives of UNESCO and the Uzbek Ministry of Cultural Affairs, and other organisations such as Heritage Central Asia, are now addressing these issues through constructive support programs for the old surviving potters.

The shadow of the Ulugbeg Madrasa (theological college) falls on the Shir-dor Madrasa opposite, on the eastern side of the Registan in Samarkand, central Uzbekistan.
PHOTO BY CHRISTINA SUMNER, 2003

From west to north-east

Wedding headdress (*kashitillo*) from about 1900 which emphasised the wearer's eyes. Silver jewellery was produced mainly by Tajik craftsmen who established workshops in the urban centres of Uzbekistan.

SILVER GILT, MOTHER-OF-PEARL, CORAL, COLOURED GLASS, ENAMEL AND COTTON THREADS, TASHKENT, UZBEKISTAN. 14 X 25 CM. STATE MUSEUM OF APPLIED ARTS, TASHKENT, UZBEKISTAN, KP5126 375-XX

The state museums of Karakalpakstan and Kazakhstan hold significant collections of textiles and ceramics. Their inclusion in this publication is important as they respectively mark the entry point of the glazed ceramic tradition into western Central Asia from the south-west and its furthermost penetration into the east and north-east. The technology of making glazed ceramics originated in China and had travelled westwards along the Silk Road trading routes to Iran long before the emergence of Islam. As Islam expanded into Central Asia with the Arabs in the eighth century, ceramic technology went too, travelling back into Central Asia where it rapidly took root. From there it moved relatively quickly in both easterly and more northerly directions. Fine tenth-century examples of Samanid wares have been found in a number of archaeological sites in Kazakhstan.

Of interest to both Guy Petherbridge and me has been the mass of evidence of design continuities and production complementarities between embroidery and ceramics, as well as works in other media. While embroidery has been almost entirely the work of women, glazed ceramic production is predominantly the work of men. Although both Kazakhs and Karakalpaks are traditionally nomadic cultures and this study primarily considers the products of oasis cultures, the broad complementarity of gender-based production in embroidery and ceramics is equally applicable. Similarly, design continuities are as evident in the ceramics and embroidery of Karakalpakstan and Kazakhstan as they are in the classic oasis cities of eastern Uzbekistan and Tajikistan, to which suzani-making is traditionally confined. Our intention has been to reflect as much of Central Asia as possible, to be inclusive rather than exclusive. However, the marvellous opus of nomadic embroidery, including Turkmen, Lakai Uzbek and Kyrgyz is beyond the scope of this publication.

Personal and professional

A young woman from Bukhara or Samarkand with her child. She wears a complete set of wedding jewellery in the highly decorative style worn by wealthy urban women of the region in the late 1800s. The wide sleeves of her ikat robe are typical of traditional dress.

REPRODUCED FROM J KALTER AND M PAVALOI, *HEIRS TO THE SILK ROAD: UZBEKISTAN*, THAMES AND HUDSON, LONDON, 1997.

The opportunity to enter and partake of another culture, however briefly and superficially, is both rewarding and affirming. My own experience of working in Central Asia has been via four all-too-brief official missions characterised by meetings, communicating through interpreters, hurried collection inspections, old Russian aeroplanes, break-neck car rides, early mornings and many unknowns. Simultaneously, these visits have been lit by the foundation and growth of lasting friendships, developing relationships with other museum professionals which I hope will bear much fruit in seasons to come, and kindness and warm hospitality from Nukus to Bukhara, Samarkand and Tashkent, from Dushanbe to Almaty.

Differences always abound between people of differing cultural and social inheritance, in attitudes to power for example, in gender relations and religion. There are however as many commonalities in ordinary everyday human experience, such as shared jokes and shared meals, a mutual understanding and enjoyment of the beauty of embroidered textiles and glazed ceramics, the pleasure of being everywhere surrounded by flowers. Indelible memories of Central Asia remain with me: late snow on cherry blossoms in Tashkent; pomegranates and persimmons; flying over the lofty Pamirs as they marched to the horizon; sharing a park bench with a stranger one golden late summer evening, together soaking up the glories of the Registan square in Samarkand. □

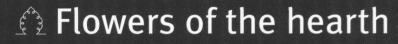

Flowers of the hearth

textiles

Christina Sumner

SUZANIS, THE FABULOUS EMBROIDERED cloths of western Central Asia, are among the world's finest and most beautiful textiles. Desired and acquired by the most ardent of textile connoisseurs, these large flower-strewn cloths were traditionally made at home by urban Uzbek and Tajik women, the inheritors of very different ancient cultures. Centuries of close contact in a shared environment gave rise however to a unified art form. The term suzani derives from *suzan*, the Farsi word for needle, and is used generically to describe a particular family of embroideries as well as specifically to describe some of the largest of these which are mainly used as wall hangings. That suzanis are as much flowers of the heart as of the domestic hearth is clearly apparent in their beauty, in the care lavished on their execution, and in their enduring cultural and personal significance to their makers and users.

While suzanis form a discrete group of embroideries and are appreciated as such, they are more deeply understood as an integral part of the embroidery traditions, both urban and nomadic, of the region as a whole. All the diverse peoples of Central Asia—Karakalpak, Kazakh, Kyrgyz, Tajik, Turkmen and Uzbek—traditionally decorate their household textiles and their clothing with embroidery. Differences, some obvious and some subtle, in the choice of materials and techniques, form and motif convey to the observer the origin of a piece and the cultural identity of its maker. The suzanis of the oasis towns of Uzbekistan and Tajikistan, for example, differ in form and ornament from the *tuskiz* of the once nomadic Kazakhs and Kyrgyz, although both are embroidered in silk on cotton, serve as wall decorations, and feature designs that rely strongly on vegetal or floral motifs.

The pairing of embroidery with glazed ceramics in this publication has been prompted by their shared preoccupation with floral imagery and their shared traditional context of domestic production. Suzanis and ceramics are also complementary in that their manufacture is gender-based—embroidery is mostly worked by women, glazed ceramics are mostly the work of men—and both have characteristic and complementary palettes: commonly warm reds and cool blues respectively. The geographic production areas of suzanis and glazed ceramics differ. Suzanis were made in an area of present-day Uzbekistan and Tajikistan that stretches roughly from Bukhara in the west to the Ferghana Valley in the east, from Tashkent in the north to Shakhrisabz and Dushanbe in the south. The glazed ceramic tradition however, as described by Guy Petherbridge in his chapter, covers a much larger area. Our inclusion of textiles from Karakalpakstan in the west and Kazakhstan in the north-east mirrors the passage of Islam and the distribution of glazed ceramics across western Central Asia. In addition these Karakalpak and Kazakh embroideries, which stem from nomadic traditions and differ markedly from the suzani forms, may remind us of the brilliance of nomadic embroidery and the interdependent relationship that has always existed between the settled and nomadic populations of the region.

Ancient traditions, aesthetic legacies

Central Asia's embroidery and glazed ceramics are the inheritors of ancient craft traditions that embrace a wide range of other media, including wood and *ganch* (plaster) carving, decorative brassware, weaving, block printing, jewellery, leatherwork and wall painting. Although suzanis have sometimes been characterised through the ethnographic lens as folk art, they have greater historical depth than this description implies. Rather, they are an evolving expression of ancient aesthetic and technological traditions. Suzanis and glazed ceramics remain an integral part of the region's cultural identity and a source of national pride.

The antiquity of textile production in Central Asia is well-documented in archaeological and textual evidence, beginning with the early production of cotton. While textiles are not generally known for their longevity (unlike ceramics), silk is remarkably resilient and a number of varied and beautiful pre-Islamic silks have been recovered from ancient burial sites along the Silk Road. The antiquity of

Amuletic ornament (*haykel*) worn as part of traditional dress by young Karakalpak women. The horizontal cylinder was used as a container for Koranic texts, other protective prayers or amulets. The finials above the amulet holder are shaped like curving rams horns. The ram was believed to be endowed with special powers.

SILVER GILT, CHASED AND SET WITH CORNELIANS, FILIGREE, MADE BY A KARAKALPAK SILVERSMITH IN KARAKALPAKSTAN, 1880-1920.
35 X 22.5 CM

Previous page: detail of a *nimsuzani*. See page 43

Detail of a wall painting at Afrasiab (ancient Samarkand), portraying men wearing silk robes patterned with ornamental roundels, rosettes and birds.
REPRODUCED FROM *AFRASIAB PAINTINGS*, UZBEK SSR ACADEMY OF SCIENCES

chain-stitch embroidery, common in suzanis, is evidenced by wall and floor coverings and costume accessories such as a wool and silk fragment with curling floral ornament from a tomb in Yinpin, Xinjiang, that may be as early as the third century BCE. The tenacity of these traditions is also clear in nomadic embroideries such as the embroidered felts of Pazyryk from the fourth to third century BCE, which so closely resemble contemporary Kazakh and Kyrgyz felts.

The region's oasis cities had long been involved in trade, and by the second century BCE the Silk Road linking China with the classical world, Iran and India were well-established. By the third century CE the Sassanians of Iran had developed a weave with patterned roundels and scrolling plant-like forms not unlike the designs of suzanis from the 1800s and 1900s. Similarly patterned silks can be seen in the sixth to eighth century frescoes of ruined Afrasiab (ancient Samarkand) and Penjikent which were built by the Sogdians, long-time inhabitants of the region. Chinese sources mentioning brocades from Samarkand and weaving utensils found at Penjikent suggest that these were locally produced. Merv, Bukhara and Samarkand were principal producers of cotton and woollen fabrics from the ninth century through to the 1200s, when the region was devastated by Mongol invasions. The splendid patterned fabrics portrayed in the Timurid miniatures of the 1300s and 1400s indicate that production and consumption were flourishing at that time.

Amir Said Alim Khan ruled the Emirate of Bukhara from 1911 until 1920, and was reknowned for his fine clothes and luxurious lifestyle. When a detachment of Bolshevik troops entered the city and stormed his palace, Said Alim Khan fled to Kabul where he died in 1944.
PHOTO BY SERGEI MIKHAILOVICH PROKUDIN-GORSKI, 1911

The legacy of 1000 years of ideas and commodities moving along the Silk Road inevitably left its mark. Cross-cultural influences on the design and techniques of extant suzanis are evident, particularly those from Persian carpets, Mughal and Ottoman embroideries and Chinese embroidery and painted porcelains. The strong design relationship to Indian textiles can be seen in the layout of some of the embroideries, the similarity of suzani blooms to their flowering ornamentation, and the frequent appearance of the ancient *boteh* motif, locally identified as a *bodum* or almond.

In addition to Zoroastrian and Buddhist influences, the advent of Islam with Arab traders at the beginning of the eighth century increasingly affected the region, its people and their arts. The area became more narrowly Islamic, particularly in the period immediately before the Russian invasions of the late 1700s and 1800s. Representations of infinity, through repetition of motif and pattern, are characteristic of Islamic art in general. Most of the suzanis still in existence date from the 1800s and

Typical of Islamic art, tile work in the Shakhi-Zinda (Living King) necropolis near Samarkand reflects a love of geometry and represents infinity through the repetition of pattern and motif.

PHOTO BY CHRISTINA SUMNER, 1999

BRIGHT FLOWERS

early 1900s, during which period the khanates (dominions) of western Central Asia were violently incorporated into the Russian empire, later to become part of the Soviet Union. Throughout these political changes, traditional Islamic culture was largely maintained.

Examination of suzanis reveals a number of similarities to different forms of textiles and other media found in the region. Grid patterns for example, which organise the central field of many suzanis, are often seen in early silks as well as in Turkish, Caucasian and Persian carpets, and wall paintings.

Domestic context of production

The blank earth-coloured exterior of a traditional Central Asian home excludes the outsider, psychologically as well as physically, in striking contrast to the richness and warmth of the interior. Externally, the most characteristic decorative feature tends to be the roofline where ornamental drainpipes occasionally add a rakish quality to the otherwise sober façade. Tall slender *terak* (poplar) trees line the streets in front of the houses, providing welcome shade. When a son is born, enough *terak* are planted to build him a house when he marries. Once within the walls another world opens up, of courtyard gardens and generous hospitality, water poured over the hands, velvet-covered *kurpatcha* (quilts), bowls of tea, bread broken and placed around the table, dishes of nuts and sweets.

In upper-class dwellings, there were two courtyards. Behind the entrance was the main courtyard (*selamlik*), where family life was centred. Leading off was a second, similar courtyard reserved for the women (*haremlik*) where only the master of the house and (with his permission) close male blood relations were allowed. In the heat of the Central Asian summer, women spent much of their day in the courtyard garden with its shady vine-covered pergolas and riot of flowers. One serene family courtyard I visited in Tashkent is planted with the three trees that are said to grow in paradise—fig, persimmon and pomegranate. Within the *haremlik* a woman was entitled to a room of her own, over which she had complete authority. Although working together on silkworm raising and embroidery for the common economic welfare of the family unit, the women of the household competed with each other for their husband's attention and sought to make or (if wealthy) buy the finest suzanis for decorating the walls. The need to keep women secluded from male guests meant that the reception room was situated near the entrance. This room, the public face of the family, was usually hung with fine suzanis or carpets. Today, most homes have a single courtyard where family and guests mingle more easily, but a clear distinction still remains between public and private spaces.

Embroidered hangings were required decoration in the homes of the settled population of the region. Rooms were largely without furniture, which is still the case in traditionally decorated homes, with the exception of a carved and painted *sanduk*, or dowry chest piled high with *kurpatcha* and *kurpa* (quilted blankets) and covered with an embroidered cloth. *Mihrab* (arch-shaped) wall niches held a range of household objects sometimes covered with an embroidered *choishab* (curtain). In

Flowers, vegetables and herbs grow in profusion in the shady inner courtyard of a typical Islamic family home in Shakhrisabz. The day bed, often piled with comfortable quilts and cushions is the centre of family life.
PHOTO BY CHRISTINA SUMNER, 2003

upper-class homes, ceilings and columns were carved and painted in bright colours and the spaces between the wall niches were painted with images of flowering shrubs. This aesthetic preference for colour and pattern endures undiminished, although in the contemporary urban apartments of Tashkent and Dushanbe, Nukus, Bukhara and Samarkand, polished cabinets and western-style seating now take pride of place and are preferred components of the dowry.

Women, marriage and Islam

Suzanis were (and in some regions such as Bukhara and Urgut still are) essential ingredients of a dowry, proof of a girl's needlework skills and marriageability, and a demonstration of her economic value to her husband's family. Marriage was the prescribed path for a young girl, though probably not to a man of her own choosing. It was not unusual for a girl to be married at twelve and be a mother by fourteen. The lowly status of the women of Central Asia in the 1800s is in marked contrast to the autonomy many women of the region enjoy today.

Girls were mostly restricted to the women's quarters of the family home from the onset of puberty. They were rarely literate and thus largely ignorant of the content of their brothers' Islamic education. Cultural transmission among women was mainly oral, from mother to daughter, and incorporated ancient apotropaic (protective) and shamanistic elements which were contrary to conventional Islamic beliefs. However women's ritual lives included ceremonies to promote good health and fertility which were dedicated to the Lady Fatima and other Islamic saints.

The lives of women in sedentary communities were in stark contrast to those of their nomad sisters, who were not veiled and often owned their yurts (felt tents). Early accounts of the *paranja* (women's veiling cloak) and *chachvan* (horsehair veil) are not appealing, but many later *paranjas* were intentionally decorative, made from brilliant ikats and figured velvets that outwardly expressed the wearer's hidden charms. The veil was eventually outlawed by the Soviets during the 1930s, a profound social change which was initially greeted with outrage.

There is a strong contrast between the inferior position once endured by many married women and the extraordinary beauty and brightness of their suzanis, into which were carefully stitched their hopes and dreams for their daughters' happiness. These glorious embroideries may be seen as triumphs of the human spirit in a society that was not egalitarian and where women's circumstances varied greatly. All were however subject to Islamic law and its restrictive codes of behaviour. Whereas men in Central Asia today still take care of all affairs outside the home, women prevail at home.

Dowries are women's work

Shortly after the birth of a baby, the parents started getting ready for their child's eventual entry into adulthood. The elaborate preparations for a daughter's wedding required the production of a number of dowry embroideries of differing form and function. Each daughter was taught to sew from an early age and was expected to make a substantial contribution towards her own dowry, if only the smaller pieces. Sometimes more distantly related women were called in to help complete the embroideries in time for the wedding. Dowry textiles were deemed to have magical properties related to protection, fertility and the birth of sons, and were a significant presence at weddings as bridal canopies and marriage-bed sheets.

The type and quantity of embroidery required for a dowry varied from region to region and with levels of prosperity. All were part of traditional interior decoration. Such embroideries are still dowry prerequisites for Uzbek and Tajik brides today and continue to serve a significant ceremonial role in wedding celebrations.

The day after a wedding in Urgut, near Samarkand, the bride's dowry is glimpsed behind a curtain. A new suzani covers the quilts and blankets (*kurpatcha* and *kurpa*) piled on top of the dowry chest (*sanduk*) and an embroidered frieze (*zardevor*) is hung at ceiling height.

PHOTO BY CHRISTINA SUMNER, 2003

Suzani making is a living heritage. In central Uzbekistan today, every girl is expected to know at least one type of handwork. Once married, she may be required to take up the craft practised by her husband's mother, since patrilocal residence is still traditionally practised in much of Central Asia. A woman lives with her husband's family when she marries and her relationship with her mother-in-law is critical to her happiness in her new home. In the past, contact with her family of origin might well be severely limited after marriage, so the suzanis the bride brought with her had emotional as well as symbolic relevance as they embodied the love and hopes of her family. Inscriptions and dates are very rare, though on one notable piece from Urgut is embroidered 'This *bolinpush* [pillow cover] delights the eye and will bring happiness to its owner'.

Different forms, different functions

Together with the 'classic' suzani or large wall hanging, the corpus of urban domestic embroidery includes smaller wall hangings, wedding-bed sheets, pillow covers, cradle covers, table covers, niche curtains, friezes and prayer mats, each of which is an essential part of traditional interior decoration. Other embroideries include *oina kalta* (mirror bags), *shona kalta* (comb bags), belts and towels, and caps for men, women and children. While much of the embroidery is done at home by the family, some items are also bought at the bazaar or from a professional embroiderer.

The particular pieces required for a girl's dowry varied from region to region. In Bukhara for example, a suzani, *nimsuzani* (half-size hanging or cover), *ruijo* or wedding-bed sheet and *joinamaz* (prayer mat) were commonly part of the dowry. The *joinamaz*, with its *mihrab*-(arch) shaped centre, was an important inclusion as devout Muslims were required to pray five times a day. In Nurata, the dowry consisted of two suzanis, two *nimsuzanis*, two *joinamaz*, two *takiapush* and two

In the Samarkand synagogue in the early 1900s, locally made suzanis and table covers and ikat hangings from Bukhara were plentiful. Most of the silk dyeing for embroidery and weaving was carried out by the Jewish community.
PHOTO FROM THE INDIGENOUS JEWISH MUSEUM COLLECTION, MUNICIPAL MUSEUM, SAMARKAND.

sandalpush. The *takiapush* is a pillow cover for the bride's bed, and was called *bolinpush* in Bukhara and Samarkand and *yastikpush* in Shakhrisabz and Tashkent. A *sandalpush* was laid over the *sandal*, a low wide table on top of a charcoal brazier; in winter, cold hands and feet were warmed by putting them under the *sandalpush*. In Tashkent, two different wall hangings were traditionally required, a *palyak* and a *gulkurpa*, together with two *choishab* or niche curtains, a *kirpech* or narrow niche curtain and a *zardevar* (frieze). The *choishab* was originally used as a marriage-bed sheet and, like the *ruijo* of Bukhara and Dushanbe, had an arch-shaped inner area; its unembroidered end was hidden under the pillow but now, when the *choishab* is hung, this is covered with the *zardevar*. Generally speaking, the positioning of embroideries in a household was determined by tradition.

When a girl marries in Tashkent or Pskent, four girlfriends will traditionally hold a *palyak* above her head to protect her from evil spirits; when she enters her husband's house, this cloth is hung on the wall as part of her dowry. Until the early 1900s, during the wedding ceremony the bride and groom were wrapped in a *gulkurpa*. In Samarkand, the bride was completely covered with a suzani for the journey from her own home to that of her bridegroom, indicative of their powerful protective function. During the wedding celebrations, the walls of the bride's room were covered with suzanis and displays of decorative embroidery were also important for holidays and festivals. Suzanis were hung and used as covers in both religious and secular public spaces used for widely different purposes, such as official and government buildings, clubs and libraries, voting booths during elections, and Jewish synagogues. Suzanis may also have served as screens so women would not be seen by men other than their husbands and close family.

Bukhara embroidery of the 1800s

Koryogdi Jurayevich Jumaev

SURVIVING CENTRAL ASIAN embroideries of the 1700s housed in collections at the Hermitage Museum in St Petersburg and the Moscow Kremlin Armoury bear witness to the skills of embroiderers from the Bukhara region. The antiquity of the tradition is confirmed by archaeological finds, as illustrated by a description dating from the early 1400s found in the Samarkand palace of Amir Timur. Large numbers of Bukhara embroideries from the 1800s are preserved in public and private collections worldwide.

The city of Bukhara is one of the oldest trade centres of Asia and, like Samarkand, was a major Silk Road city. Bukhara was frequently conquered, the last major invaders being the Uzbek Turks, following the dissolution of the Timurid Empire in the 1500s. In the 1700s fighting between rival Uzbek leaders led to the establishment of the khanates of Khiva and Kokand and in 1750, the Emirate of Bukhara. The emirate comprised much of present-day Uzbekistan, Tajikistan and Turkmenistan, its population largely a mixture of urban Tajiks and often nomadic Turkic peoples. This balance remained until well into the 1900s. Bukhara was renowned for its decorative arts, with a quarter of its population working as artisans. The city, also like Samarkand, boasted a heritage of brilliant religious architecture and was known as a centre for Islamic studies.

As part of their expansion into Central Asia, the Russians declared Bukhara a protectorate in 1868 which it remained until 1917 when the last amir, Alim Khan, declared independence. Three years later, Bukhara was taken by the Russian Bolsheviks, who established the People's Soviet Republic of Bukhara with a population of Tajiks, Uzbeks, Turkmen, Kyrgyz and Kazakhs. The slow process of separating these Central Asian peoples into different regions then began. Eventually the Republic of Bukhara was divided up, the major part becoming the SSR of Uzbekistan.

The Bukhara school of embroidery

Embroidery with silk threads on cotton was widespread among the settled population of the towns and villages between the Amu Darya and Syr Darya. A significant national art form, these embroideries called suzanis were created by women for domestic use and as essential components of their daughters' dowries. Suzanis worked in and around Bukhara became the dominant style throughout the emirate, although regional centres, such as Nurata, Shakhrisabz, Samarkand and especially Tashkent and Pskent, evolved their own distinctive forms. The highpoint of Bukhara embroidery production was between 1850 and 1920, when Bukhara was the capital and leading artistic centre of the emirate.

By the end of the 1800s, the Bukhara school of embroidery was concentrated in three main centres, Gizduvan, Shafirkhan and Vabkent. Many of the embroideries classified as Bukharan were in fact produced in Shafirkhan, one of the largest centres of embroidery situated about 25 kilometres north-east of Bukhara. Suzanis from Shafirkhan were worked in chain stitch, often on a coloured ground with a preference for natural forms; their motifs leaned towards the floral and zoomorphic. The medieval city of Gizduvan contributed significantly to the Bukhara school, producing suzanis similar in style to those from Bukhara itself but which were noted for their originality, composite forms and contrasting colours. Later embroideries from Gizduvan were worked on coloured cloth. While stylistically similar to embroideries from Bukhara and Gizduvan, those from Vabkent are best known for their unique decorative qualities and choice of colours.

Prior to the 1900s the attribution of an embroidery to Bukhara referred not only specifically to the town and its environs, but also to the wider region of the Emirate, and later Republic, of Bukhara.

DETAIL FROM A *JOMA* (MAN'S COAT) BUKHARA, UZBEKISTAN, c1894–95. SEE PAGE 46

Virtually every Uzbek or Tajik urban or village household produced a range of dowry embroideries. If a girl and the women of her family were unable to finish an embroidery in time for her wedding, they were entitled to ask for help (*hashar*) from their relatives and neighbours. Houses were decorated, not only on special occasions, with large and small wall hangings (suzanis and *nimsuzanis*), pillow covers (*takiapush*, *bolinpush* or *yastikpush*), wedding-bed sheets (*joipush*, *ruijo* or *choishab*), prayer mats (*joinamaz*), covers for stoves (*sandalpush*) and bags for numerous small objects such as mirrors and combs. Costumes including the cloak-like *paranja*, dresses, jackets, trousers and robes were often decorated with embroidery, especially at the collar and hem, and were also hung in the rooms for decorative purposes.

During the mid 1800s changes in the economic and social conditions of the emirate created a climate in which professional embroidery could also flourish. This period saw the development of couched gold thread embroidery (*zarduzi*), originally created to serve the needs of the amir and his court, but later expanding to produce luxury commodities for a wider market in the late 1800s. In both court and private workshops, professional male needleworkers embroidered elaborate gold and silver hangings, exquisite robes, horse covers, caps, head-dresses and other small accessories.

The Bukhara suzani

The most significant type of embroidery produced in the Bukhara region was the suzani itself—a large, prestigious and lavishly embroidered panel used as a wall decoration or as a bedcover for a newly married couple to protect them from harm. The term suzani, which comes from the Farsi *suzan* for needle, is only used for large embroideries and not for embroidery on clothes or other objects. A distinctive feature of Bukharan suzanis is the masterful use of chain stitch (*yurma*), worked on handwoven cotton (*karbos*) or a coarse linen (*biaz*), with either a needle or a tambour hook. Basma, often referred to as Bukhara couching, was also widely used. Large surfaces of the cloth were typically covered leaving only small areas of background free. The brilliant colours of the silk and the use of natural motifs created a field of magnificent, almost iridescent flowering forms enhanced by the contrasting texture of the different types of stitching.

Thematically, Bukharan suzanis were mainly based on vegetal forms, with a preference for slender flowering branches and circular rosettes (*doiragul*), and including some household objects such as kitchen knives transformed into curving leaves. The *islimi* pattern was usually placed along the borders, an undulating stem carrying flower buds symbolising the renewal of life. The decorative motifs also reflect the architectural ornament of Bukhara's medieval monuments. Most suzani motifs carried symbolic meaning relating to fertility, protection, health and household stability.

Suzani design, which was drawn on the cloth by the community's specialist designer, the *shizmakash* or *kalamkash*, relies on the placement of ornamental elements in the central field and a wide border as a frame. Although generally similar, we can identify five principal types with the addition of compound compositions. These are:

1. tree (*daraht*) patterns in which the central field features tree-like forms growing from bottom to top; branches with flowers, leaves and other vegetal elements spread out from the main trunk. The centre is framed by a succession of narrow and wide borders, richly ornamented with vegetal motifs
2. rhythmically placed rosettes on a central field, enhanced by a wide border of similar elements, with the centre sometimes accentuated by a larger rosette
3. a diagonal grid (*tabondi*) is formed by leafy motifs creating rhomboid cells in which decorative motifs such as flowers, butterflies and birds are placed
4. a strong central rosette (*doiragul*) or star-like form (*tupbargul*), composed of the traditional vegetal elements within a complex composition that entirely covers the background. The placement of the secondary elements varies, sometimes distributed without an underlying rhythm and sometimes creating complex geometric patterns
5. 'large medallion' suzanis, in which a complex centred design covers the entire inner surface; the borders are narrow but otherwise similar.

The wedding-bed sheet (*joipush*)

The second major type of embroidery produced in the Bukhara region was the bedspread or wedding-bed sheet (*joipush* or *ruijo*, known as *choishab* in Tashkent). The basic design is an upside down U, creating an arched form similar to the mihrab of the prayer mat (*joinamaz*) with embroidery across the top and down both sides. The embroidery motifs on *joipush* varied, but were typically massed flowers including rosettes (*doiragul*), almonds (*bodum*),

DETAIL FROM A *NIMSUZANI* (SMALL WALL HANGING) FROM THE BUKHARA REGION, UZBEKISTAN, LATE 1800s ILLUSTRATING ONE OF JUMAEV'S PRINCIPAL TYPES (POINT 4). SEE PAGE 45

seven-coloured blossoms (*guli hafrang*), ivy (*savsangul*), leafy sprays (*hibcha navda*) and cherries (*gilosak*).

Carrying diverse symbolic messages, *joipush* and suzani celebrated women's creativity and the transmission of skills to their daughters. In addition to its obvious decorative value in the home, embroidery embodied important community traditions and was an essential accompaniment to rituals surrounding both weddings and funerals. During a wedding embroideries played a ritual part in covering the bridal bed and decorating the walls of the wedding chamber. Afterwards *joipush* were used as bed coverings and were folded away during the day, while large suzanis were stored in chests and only taken out to decorate the house on special occasions. At funerals, an embroidery was used to cover the bier (*tobut*) holding the body of a young woman or girl who had died before marriage.

A small section of a suzani was always left unfinished, perhaps to ensure that 'there will continue to be weddings in the home', and to 'have a daughter alive, so that happiness at home never ends'. □

Regional styles

By the late 1800s and early 1900s, important centres of embroidery were well-established in Nurata, Bukhara, Samarkand, Shakhrisabz, Tashkent and Ferghana. The quality of the embroidery, the complexity of the production process and the sophistication of the design repertoire testify that the tradition had developed over a long period of time. Although the embroideries produced in these centres appear to have identifiable regional characteristics, they must be considered as broad generalisations as the correct attribution of suzanis is notoriously difficult in the absence of provenance.

For example, the magnificent suzanis of Bukhara often feature stylised and highly ornamental rosettes in soft reds, pinks and blues on slender branches evenly distributed over the field; they have

Mrs Kubaro Tokhtaeva embroiders a pillow cover in her Urgut home. Behind her is a precious family suzani, worked for her by her mother-in-law Mrs Sakhobat Rakhmatillaeva in the early 1980s as a wedding present.
PHOTO BY CHRISTINA SUMNER, 2003

wide borders, often feature *islimi* (scrolling plant) patterns and are distinguished by their skillful use of chain stitch. Those from Shakhrisabz feature richly ornamental central rosettes, with smaller rosettes, leafy garlands and the *chor chirog* (four lamp) motif. Suzanis from Samarkand are brightly coloured but have narrow borders and may feature more geometric roundels or rosettes surrounded by vigorous leafy circles and scrolls. Suzanis from nearby Urgut all now include the spouted jug or *choinak*, symbol of hospitality and respect for guests. Suzanis of typical Nurata style have narrow borders with sprays of delicate naturalistic flowers growing from the corners and sides towards a flower-filled star in the centre. Those from Bukhara, Shakhrisabz and Nurata bear the closest relationship to Persian and Mughal designs.

Palyak from the Tashkent area are nearly square, their surfaces almost entirely covered with embroidery; they usually feature large red circular *oi* (moon) motifs, whereas earlier floral examples were more finely decorated. Those from neighbouring Pskent include more yellow embroidery and the large motifs are typically star-shaped. *Gulkurpa* on the other hand have a central floral star motif surrounded by more flowers, although earlier examples demonstrate a much closer design relationship to the suzani—probably indicating common ancestry. Further east in the Ferghana Valley, it is difficult to evaluate a regional character for suzanis, probably because of the region's exposure to centuries of foreign influences. *Ruijo* are common however, and brightly coloured concentric rings and slender branches are typically worked on coloured ground cloth with tightly twisted silks, leaving much of the background free.

While pattern types can be loosely linked to particular localities, many embroideries combine elements from different regions. These overlaps may reflect the proximity of embroidery centres or an exchange of embroideries in a circumscribed production area. They probably also reflect the relocation of women to their husband's family home upon marriage, bringing them into immediate contact with the embroidery styles of their mother-in-law and her *kalamkash* (designer). Although a woman might embroider the preferred designs of her new locality, she usually continued to use the embroidery techniques learned from her own mother.

The kalamkash (designer), flowers and symbols

The role of the gifted women who became *kalamkash* was highly valued and skills were often passed from mother to daughter. Certain key embroideries were preserved within communities and some households were regarded as the traditional keepers of significant patterns and symbols. These were used as an important source of imagery, although the design of each individual suzani was unique. Designs were strongly traditional, following a time-honoured canon, and were often shamanistic, carrying an intention to promote the health, prosperity and fertility of the bridal couple. The *kalamkash* developed the basic composition of the design by folding the ground cloth lengthways, crossways and diagonally and marking the major points; she then drew directly onto the cloth freehand, sometimes using plates or bowls to outline the rosettes. Traditionally, older women advised against a woman being both embroiderer and designer as this was believed to cause unhappiness.

Typically, suzani designs have a central field surrounded by a border or series of borders, thus bearing a strong resemblance to locally produced carpets. Most suzanis reveal ideas derived from a range of sources as well as an inherent sense of order, while characteristic irregularities simultaneously bring flavour, lightness and interest to the overall balance. While flowers and leaves are the principal ornaments in suzanis, not surprisingly in a long-established agricultural economy, most flowers are highly abstracted and their identity consequently uncertain. Others however are more recognisable as carnations, irises, roses and tulips. Courtyard gardens filled with flowers are to be found within most family compounds, and in the spring many roofs are covered with carpets of poppies, but it seems likely that flowers were internalised by the *kalamkash* and their essence expressed by her, rather than drawn from nature. Suzanis from Nurata come closest to naturalistic representation. Stylistically, the flower motifs on suzanis are often reminiscent of Ottoman embroidery, Persian carpets and Indian *palempores* (painted and dyed cotton wall hangings or coverlets), which is indicative of both the longevity of the tradition and the cross-cultural influences that formed them.

Mrs Rajabbiy Kholova, suzani designer (*kalamkash*) in Urgut, standing in front of a suzani recently designed and worked by her. Mrs Kholova began practising as a *kalamkash* shortly after her marriage 40 years ago.
PHOTO CHRISTINA SUMNER, 2003

Elaborate rosette forms predominate, transmuting into decorative roundels in the Samarkand region and striking plain red circles in Tashkent. The circle is an archaic and recurrent motif common to many traditions and probably refers to the sun and the moon, whose worship was once so important in agricultural societies. The circular motifs of Samarkand suzanis have been linked to the suns and moons of ancient Sogdian art, and (I was told) also represent the local bread, which is round and flat with an impressed flower pattern in the centre. Scrolling plant and leaf forms (*islimi*), typical of Islamic art, fill the space between the rosettes and are reminiscent of similar imagery in the male decorative traditions of tile-work, wood-carving, brasswork, *ganch* and glazed ceramics. Among the flowers, a linking stem can sometimes be found suggesting the ancient tree-of-life motif that mediates between earth and heaven. Under the influence of Islam, the nomadic and Chinese animal imagery that was prevalent in the region has gradually segued into plant forms.

In addition to flowers and leaves, the *bodum* or almond motif is commonly found. Recognised elsewhere as the *boteh* motif or paisley pattern, the *bodum* signifies abundance as does the popular seed-filled *anor* (pomegranate), ancient symbol of fertility. Long narrow *bodums* are often indistinguishable from *kalumfer* (chilli peppers) whose power is protective, or apotropaic, like that of the curving elongated *kordi osh* (the distinctive Central Asian kitchen knife) and *chor chirog* (four-spouted lamp) motifs (although the latter has recently been related to a pattern common in Chinese porcelain of the late 1600s). Often abstracted and disguised among the foliage, tiny symbolic forms sometimes appear: a small *oftoba* (water jug) representing life-giving water and ritual purity, birds (traditionally viewed as images of the soul, mediators between earth and heaven and having prophetic significance), and fish. A triangular motif representing the *tumor* (an amulet associated with women) is also frequently worked; charms and amulets were considered essential and were both worn and kept in the home.

These talismanic devices—reflecting pre-Islamic symbolism and the eternal significance of fire and light—were embroidered into suzanis as protection against harm. Both household fire and the fire of the sun are implicit in the large circular astrological motifs of Tashkent and Pskent. Although the meanings of these ancient symbols have been substantially lost, the motifs are still embroidered for their familiarity and decorative qualities.

Cotton, silk and colour

Typically, suzani makers (and other Central Asian embroiderers) use brightly coloured silk threads to work their decorative magic on plain cotton ground cloths. Cotton is inexpensive and offers a sturdy base through which a needle can be passed repeatedly without causing unacceptable damage. Silk on the other hand is expensive, its production requiring considerable investment of time and effort. Moreover, its smoothness, lustre and glorious colour-reflecting properties are ideally suited to embroidery, which adds strength as well as value to unadorned cloth. It is not uncommon to find very old stitching bright and intact on a fragile, disintegrating ground cloth.

Cotton has been grown in Central Asia since the Neolithic period. On conquering the Central Asian khanates in the late 1800s, the Russians saw clearly that cotton would play a primary role in the economy of their newly acquired territories. The best American cotton was planted on every available piece of land; with the outlawing of slavery, new employment opportunities for women opened up in the cotton fields. The importance of cotton to the economy of Central Asia today cannot be underestimated; nor, sadly, can the environmental damage in the Aral Sea area, caused by draining water from the Amu Darya (Oxus River) to irrigate the thirsty cotton fields upstream.

In October, towards the end of the cotton-picking season, an Uzbek woman stands in one of the cotton fields that line the road between Bukhara and Samarkand, searching for the last few bolls of cotton.
PHOTO BY CHRISTINA SUMNER, 2002

Travelling through present day Uzbekistan on the road to Samarkand, Bukhara and beyond, one passes acre after endless acre of cotton fields. In autumn, during the cotton harvest, the fields are dotted with pickers, their hair tied up in bright kerchiefs, their faces covered with scarves; trucks and handcarts piled high with creamy raw cotton crowd the roads and, in the outdoor state repositories, great tarpaulin-covered 'haystacks' of cotton proliferate. The symbiotic relationship between cotton and silk is apparent in the regular planting of mulberry trees along irrigation channels that border the cotton fields. Part windbreak, part soil-consolidator, and nourished by the cotton fertiliser, mulberry trees are essential for rearing silkworms, which eat only their leaves.

Until the 1880s, women embroidered their suzanis on 30 cm-wide strips of natural handwoven cotton called *karbos*, sometimes tinted light brown with tea leaves or onion skins, or on a creamy yellow cotton called *malla*. The ginning and spinning of cotton was the work of women, but in urban communities men wove the narrow plain-weave strips. After about 1880, brightly coloured factory-woven silks and cottons were imported and used as ground cloth. In the mid 1900s locally woven violet and orange cottons were added to the range of options. Today, handwoven *karbos* is once again widely used for both large suzanis and smaller projects such as cushion covers and bags for the tourist market.

Silk production originated in China some 7000 years ago, but the art of raising silkworms was not practised in western Turkestan until the first centuries CE. Thanks to its inherent splendour, and the secrecy that long surrounded its production in China, silk became a highly valued commodity that functioned much like coinage. Taxes were paid in bolts of silk, foreign dignitaries were given diplomatic gifts of silk, and the Silk Road trade was stimulated. Silk was desirable, lightweight and portable, a merchant's dream. Five major civilisations were involved in the early Silk Road trade: the Chinese, the Romans, the Parthians of Iran, the Kushans of northern India, and the nomads of the Central Asian steppes. Trade would have been impossible however without the skills, enterprise and entrepreneurial know-how of the Central Asian oasis dwellers, the Sogdians, who made a highly successful living as agriculturalists and merchants.

Silk production has always been time consuming and labour intensive. Raising silkworms was women's work and they often funded their embroidery through the sale of silk cocoons or small finished items. Unwinding the delicate silk filaments from the cocoons and the production and dyeing of silk embroidery threads was generally accomplished in all-male workshops by the long-established local Jewish communities. Today however, in the ikat factories of Margilan in the Ferghana Valley, women reel the silky filaments from scalding cocoons.

Prior to the discovery of aniline dyes in the 1850s, natural vegetable and insect dyes were used to dye the silk threads (*ipak*). These included *nil* (indigo, imported from India), *rujan* (madder) and *kirmizi* (cochineal, imported from Russia) for red, *isparak* (delphinium) for yellow, and *anor pusti* (pomegranate peel) for black. Within a few years aniline dyes were readily available in the region and thanks to their ease of use, their popularity was assured. However, aniline colours were harsh and early on were fugitive, which affected many embroideries of the latter 1800s. Between about 1850 and 1880 expensive cinnabar-red wool threads were imported from India.

The growing contemporary preference for dyeing silk embroidery threads with natural dyes indicates a return to the practices of the 1800s and earlier. Once a well-kept secret within a family, these dye recipes are now well-known. Today, women dye their silks themselves, producing soft shades of yellow from onion skin, orange from *royan* root, mauve from cherry, purple from mulberries, grey-blue from cherry and ash, brown from walnuts, grey-brown from walnut flowers, grey from *osma* leaves and ochre from the bark of the *chenar* (plane) tree.

Production and stitches

To make a large suzani in the traditional manner took around 18 months; typically they measured about 250 by 180 cm. Six narrow strips of hand-woven cotton of the desired length were loosely tacked together and the pattern drawn on the whole cloth by the *kalamkash*. The women who were to carry out the embroidery then agreed on the colours before the cloth was separated into its component strips. In present-day Shafirkhan, where suzanis are made in this traditional manner, different parts of the pattern are coded with marks representing the colours selected. Once all the strips have been embroidered, they are sewn together again to form the finished suzani. The separation of the strips for embroidery and their execution by different women accounts for the idiosyncratic differences and mismatches that characterise suzanis and contribute substantially to their charm.

Although a limited number of embroidery stitches are used in suzanis, they are worked with brilliance and subtlety and an inspired use of colour. Variations of couching and chain stitch predominate and different techniques are often found in the same piece. There are two forms of couching, *basma* and *kanda khayol*. In *basma*, the couching stitches are short, sharply angled and carefully aligned to produce a textured surface that resembles weaving. In *kanda khayol*, the couching stitches are longer and more closely aligned with the laid threads, producing a smoother surface. *Basma* was widely used in Nurata, Samarkand and Tashkent whereas in Shakhrisabz the women preferred *kanda khayol* couching.

Suzanis are valued for the fineness of their stitching, and the colour and design. Chain stitch is one of the most ancient of embroidery stitches and is worked with either needle (*nina*) or tambour hook (*daravsh*). Tambouring was often pulled unevenly, giving the chain a firmer edge on one side, which was used to great decorative effect. The terms for chain stitch can vary with technique and locality, but in the Bukhara region tamboured chain is called *yurma* and needle-worked chain stitch is called *ilmok*. Wide chain stitch, or ladder stitch, is also called *ilmok*, while chain stitch with alternate loops worked in different colours is apparently, and rather confusingly, also called *kanda khayol*. Tambour sewing machines were introduced at the end of the 1800s for the rapid commercial production of suzanis and other embroideries, and are still in use today.

Iroqi, a couched stitch with the even appearance of half cross stitch, covers the entire cloth and is restricted to the Shakhrisabz area. *Iroqi* was used to work everything from large wall hangings to horse blankets, men's robes, caps, fans and mirror bags. Today, women around Shakhrisabz (ancient Kesh

A young Tajik woman embroiders a suzani strip in a workshop recently established in their home by a couple in Shafirkhan, near Bukhara. The suzani master (*usto*) oversees the embroidery; the designs are now drawn by her husband, after receiving instruction from local women.
PHOTO BY CHRISTINA SUMNER, 2002

and the birthplace of Amir Timur or Tamerlane), are reproducing the old patterns in high quality *iroqi* embroidery, the production of which is well-organised and widely marketed. Originally, embroiderers worked their *iroqi* into handwoven *karbos*, but today, for the best work, the preferred ground fabric is *kanava*, a fine double-mesh book-binding gauze imported from Russia.

Men and embroidery

Although in a traditional domestic context embroidery was women's work, in other circumstances men also worked as embroiderers. The lavish gold embroidery for men's ceremonial robes was nearly always done by men.

Gold thread embroidery (*zarduzi*) has a long history in Central Asia. Evidence from archaeological excavations near Tashkent dates to the first and second centuries CE and Arab records of the eighth century mention the craft. *Zarduzi* reached its height at the Bukhara court in the mid 1800s, with a large workshop in the amir's residence itself and several large private workshops.

Usto Bakhshillo Jumayev, master of gold embroidery, at work in his Gold Embroidery Centre in Bukhara.

PHOTO COURTESY USTO BAKHSHILLO JUMAYEV

Gold embroidery was both precious and prestigious, and was used for ceremonial purposes. *Zarduzi* was widely understood to have been an exclusive part of urban court culture, its use restricted to the amir, his court and a few wealthy women. However a recent study has shown that gold embroidery was in fact quite widespread in a society made prosperous by trade. *Zarduzi* served as both luxury commodity and official court art until the 1920s. Court-determined conventions however were strictly observed by all who wore gold-embroidered garments and accessories. This type of embroidery, generally worked on rich dark velvets, was also greatly favoured for richly ornamental horse blankets.

The highly valued skills of the *zarduzi* master were generally handed down from father to son, although craftsmen from different traditions could also become masters. Boys generally began their apprenticeship, with some ceremony, at about the age of ten and studied for four to seven years which prepared them for setting up practice in both private and court workshops. Gold embroidery was time consuming and although mainly men's work, close women relatives were enlisted to help out when there were large orders to fulfill.

During the Soviet era, *zarduzi* production was restructured and initially appropriated for military uniforms and large banners. Women were recruited to stitch gold-embellished souvenirs and national costumes for theatre and dance. More recently, gold embroidery also ornaments women's festive dress and is found on the *peshonaband* (head dress), *peshkurta* (dress frontal), *kaltacha* (woman's coat) and *doppe* (skull cap). Factory production was also encouraged with suzanis churned out by the hundred by men using chain stitch sewing machines. Today in Uzbekistan some men have joined forces with their wives in the cottage-industry production of suzanis for both local and tourist markets. Others have taken over the significant role of *kalamkash* (designer), traditionally the exclusive work of the community's older women, drawing on museum holdings for inspiration rather than inherited imagery and cultural information passed down the female line.

Karakalpak and Kazakh embroidery

Western Uzbekistan was once known as Khorezm, through which the ancient east-west caravan routes passed. Much of the region is desert scattered with ruined forts. Today it is autonomous Karakalpakstan, its principal urban centres Khiva, Kunya Urgench and Nukus, its economy devastated by the ecological Aral Sea catastrophe. The origin of the Karakalpak people, whose earliest known mention is in the late 1500s, is uncertain. Their name means 'black cap', and their Turkic language is more akin to Kazakh than to Uzbek.

Karakalpak culture was traditionally semi-nomadic. A particular feature of their rich material culture was textiles, including finely woven carpets, bags and other decorative yurt furnishings, elaborately embroidered costume and heavy jewellery. Women's clothes varied in colour according to the age of the wearer. Girls and women of child-bearing age wore red, traditional wedding dresses (*kok koilek*) were blue, and older women wore white. The older a woman was, the less embroidery would ornament her white head covering (*ak kimishek*) and white outer robe (*ak zegde*).

Familiar with the grid-based designs of their traditional knotted carpets and tent bands, Karakalpak women embroidered their dresses and robes, bags and belts with counted-thread embroidery, the geometry of which differs markedly from the chain-stitched curves and couched rosettes of urban Tajik and Uzbek embroidery. This style of stitching has more affinity with the counted-thread embroidery of the nomadic Lakai Uzbeks, and the *iroqi* work of Shakhrisabz.

The Kazakh people, who also speak a Turkic language, inhabit the vast northern steppes of Central Asia. One arm of the Silk Road network passed through the southern cities of present-day Kazakhstan, leaving a characteristic potpourri of cultural and ideological influences. Traditionally, the Kazakhs were pastoral nomads who lived a life rich in ceremony associated with birth, childhood, marriage and death. According to Kazakh tradition, when a boy was born he was announced as *zhilkishi* (horseman), while a girl was called *kestegoi*, which refers to needlework. They lived in felt tents or yurts decorated on the inside with colourful woven, felted and embroidered carpets, covers, bags, bands and hangings made by the women. Among these were the beautiful *tuskiz*, which adorned the yurt wall and typically featured floral embroidery and designs reminiscent of the patterns on felted carpets, ancient and modern.

An embroidered *tuskiz*, whose floral roundels resemble those on the urban suzanis of western Central Asia, hangs by the men's quarter of a nomadic yurt on display in the Central State Museum of the Republic of Kazakhstan.

PHOTO BY CHRISTINA SUMNER, 2003

31

By the mid 1800s, most Kazakhs were under Russian rule. As Russian farmers planted acres of grain further southwards and Uzbek and Tajik farmers extended cultivation northwards, many Kazakhs were forced to abandon nomadism. Kazakh textiles and costume since the 1800s reflect both their nomadic inheritance and increasing cultural contact with near neighbours. The motifs and pattern of their embroideries echo the ancient designs of Pazyryk, the Silk Road legacy and floral ornament drawn from multiple sources, including suzanis.

Survival of suzanis through change

The traditional urban embroideries of Uzbekistan and Tajikistan have survived centuries of change and recurrent disruptions to their parent culture. They may have evolved into their present forms in response to the increasingly limited trade in the region as sea routes between east and west opened up

In the home of suzani master (*usto*) Mrs Mukhabat Kuchkorova in Shafirkhan, near Bukhara, bedding is neatly stored during the day on top of her dowry chest, covered with a *nimsuzani* and a prayer.
PHOTO BY CHRISTINA SUMNER, 2002

Opposite: *suzani* detail (see page 38)

in the 1500s. Silk Road traffic, other than the increasingly important trade in carpets and gemstones, decreased in consequence. There were fewer splendid textile imports to choose from and women perhaps became more dependent on their own resources and skills for the production of soft furnishings, fine caps and elegant mirror bags.

One of the features of Central Asian crafts as a whole is that the skills involved were both widely and competently practised. During the 1800s, large numbers of highly accomplished craftswomen and men were working in nearly every town and village. Records from this period indicate intensive handcraft production when villages and districts had their own craft specialisation and traditional techniques, and styles were preserved through long-established craft guilds. In the traditional bazaars where craftsmen produced and sold their goods, supply balanced demand.

With Tsarist rule in the late 1800s came an increase in cheap factory imports, which impacted negatively on the equivalent handcrafted wares. Traditional types of embroidery were not so badly affected, although the scope for embroidery production broadened from dowry and family needs to marketplace. Professional craftswomen began to create embroideries for wealthy patrons and for sale. Items produced for the markets gradually decreased in quality however; designs lost their integrity and colours their brilliance as textile workers began to use synthetic dyes. Despite this, fine examples from this brief era are indicative of the durability of the tradition.

The attainment of independence in the early 1990s brought profound changes to the traditional crafts. A resurgence of nationalism and the growth of a new market economy have helped reinstate traditional customs. Many traditional crafts, discouraged or banned during Soviet times, were revived and are now being developed with the support of government and non-government agencies. Today, the age-old skills related to architectural decoration and interior furnishings are enjoying a strong renaissance in the hands of contemporary designers and artists working in a range of media, including embroidery and glazed ceramics. A shared inherited vocabulary of imagery, pattern and motif is everywhere apparent. This predilection for traditional ornament, much of which is inspired by the bright flowers of the oases, has endured through the centuries. Then and now, it characterises Central Asian arts. □

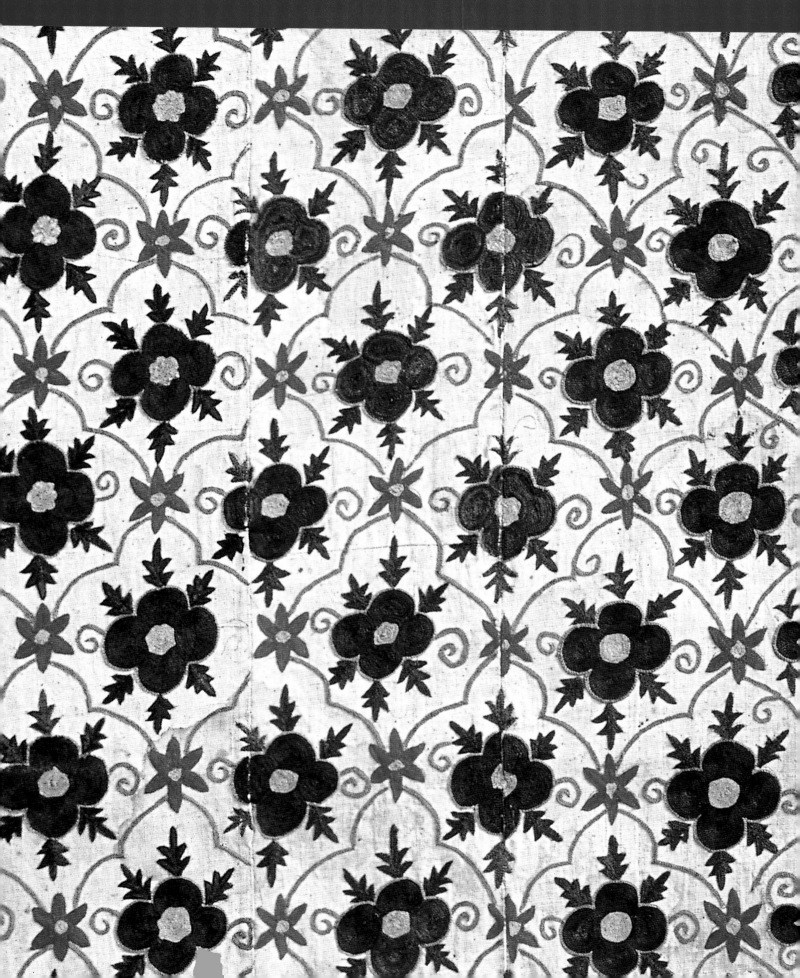

Kok koylek (wedding dress)
The *kok koylek* is a rare survivor of an old Karakalpak tradition. Typically embroidered with geometric patterns said to represent the chain mail armour of ancestral Scythian warrior women, the *kok koylek* is worn as a wedding dress with a *kizil zegde* (red robe), a *kizil kimishek* (red head covering) and a precise headdress.
● Silk cross stitch on indigo-dyed cotton, made by a Karakalpak woman in Karakalpakstan, 1880–1920. 130 x 80 cm

Kizil jipek zegde (red robe)

Red (*kizil*) outer robes with narrow sleeves and fine embroidery were worn for weddings, holidays and festivals by young Karakalpak women of marriageable age and during their child-bearing years.

● Floss silk embroidery on wool and cotton with silk braid and tassels, made by a Karakalpak woman in Karakalpakstan, 1880–1920. 147.5 x 97 cm

IV SAVITSKY STATE MUSEUM OF ART OF THE REPUBLIC OF KARAKALPAKSTAN, NUKUS, KP5812 B-448. PHOTO BY KONSTANTIN MINAYCHENKO

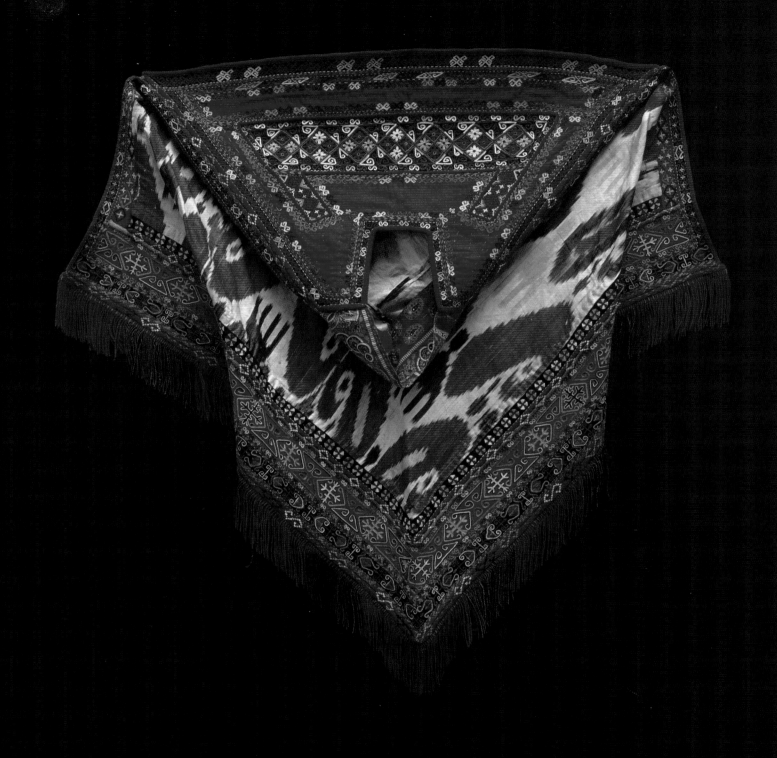

Kizil kimishek (red head covering)
Young Karakalpak girls began to make their *kizil kimishek* as children, finishing at around fourteen, in time for their wedding. The *kimishek* was effectively her diploma, evidence of her socially and economically important skills as an embroiderer. *Kimisheks* covered the head and shoulders, with fine embroidery at the front, a shawl at the back and a red turban cloth (*kizil turme*) covering the cap. After the Bolshevik revolution in the early 1920s, *kimisheks* were prohibited.

● Silk embroidery on wool with cotton cap, silk ikat panels and fringe, made by Karakalpak women in Karakalpakstan, 1880–1920. 129 x 86.5 x 80.5 cm

IV SAVITSKY STATE MUSEUM OF ART OF THE REPUBLIC OF KARAKALPAKSTAN, NUKUS, KP 10589 B-437. PHOTO BY KONSTANTIN MINAYCHENKO

Ak zegde (white robe)

Once a Karakalpak woman's child-bearing years were over, she gave away her red clothes and began to wear white (*ak*). This *ak zegde*, liberally covered with red embroidery, was worn over a dark dress and white *kimishek* by a woman just past menopause. The older she became, the less embroidery adorned her robe.

● Silk floss cross-stitch embroidery on unbleached calico, silk braid edging and printed cotton lining, made by a Karakalpak woman in Karakalpakstan, 1880–1920. 141 x 55 cm

Takiapush (pillow cover)
The *takiapush* was used initially to cover pillows on a wedding bed and later to cover quilts and blankets piled on top of the *sanduk* (dowry chest) during the day. The grid design of the central field recalls Islamic tiles, while its continuation under the surrounding borders reflects the infinity of Allah's universe.
● Silk *yurma* (tamboured chain stitch) on *karbos* (hand-woven cotton), Persian printed cotton lining, made in Shafirkhan near Bukhara, Uzbekistan, 1850–1900. 183 x 133 cm

Joipush or ruijo (wedding-bed sheet)

The *joipush* or *ruijo* was an essential component of traditional dowries in the Bukhara region of western Turkestan. This exceptional example, worked with a tambour hook (*darvash*), is from the dowry of the wife of Amir Said Alim Khan, the last Amir of Bukhara. Typical of *joipush*, the composition is in *mihrab* (arch) style.

● Silk chain stitch on cotton, silk fringe, made by Tajik or Uzbek women in the Bukhara region, Uzbekistan, late 1800s. 271 x 192 cm

BUKHARA STATE ART AND ARCHITECTURAL MUSEUM, UZBEKISTAN, KP2 1818/10. PHOTO BY KONSTANTIN MINAYCHENKO

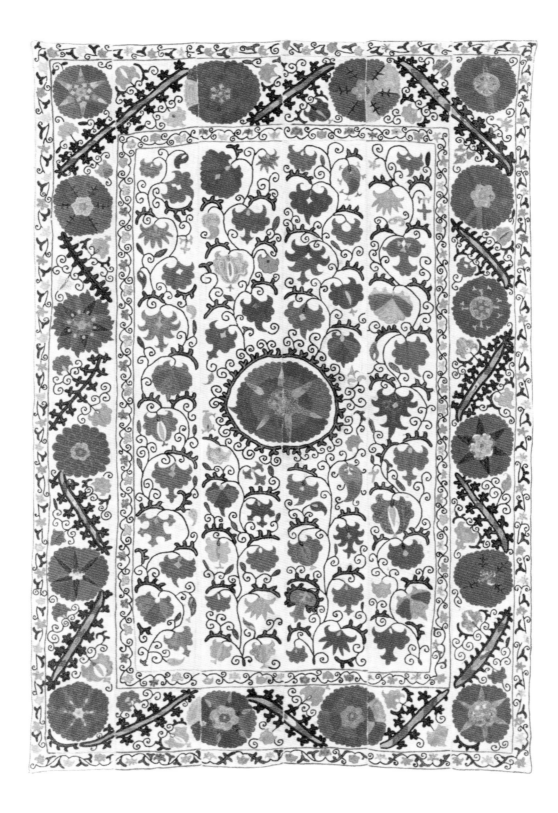

Suzani (wall hanging)
The separately embroidered strips of cloth of which suzanis are composed can be seen in this example. The central field is four strips wide, with flowering stems around a large central rosette. In the border, rosettes alternate with slender leaf forms sometimes identified as the protective (apotropaic) kitchen knife (*kordi osh*) motif. Central Asian knives curve distinctively at each end, as these motifs do, in opposite directions.
● Silk chain stitch on *karbos* (hand-woven cotton), made by a Tajik woman in the Bukhara region, Uzbekistan, about 1900. 237 x 160 cm

Suzani (wall hanging)

The flowers on this suzani are more differentiated than usual. They grow from a single stem that originates in the bottom left-hand corner of the field and is watered from a small embroidered water jug. Water jugs, symbols of the water that gives life to the oases, are often found in suzanis.

● Silk *basma* (couching) and *yurma* (chain stitch) on *karbos* (hand-woven cotton), made by Tajik or Uzbek women in the Bukhara region, Uzbekistan, early to mid 1800s. 234 x 173 cm

Takiapush (pillow cover)

The design of this embroidery from Bukhara features the ancient tree-of-life motif that recurs in Asian art across media. The *takiapush* was used to cover the pillows on the wedding bed and later to cover bedding stored away during the day.

● Silk *yurma* (chain stitch) on *karbos* (hand-woven cotton), made by a Tajik or Uzbek woman in the Bukhara region, Uzbekistan, late 1800s. 183 x 133 cm

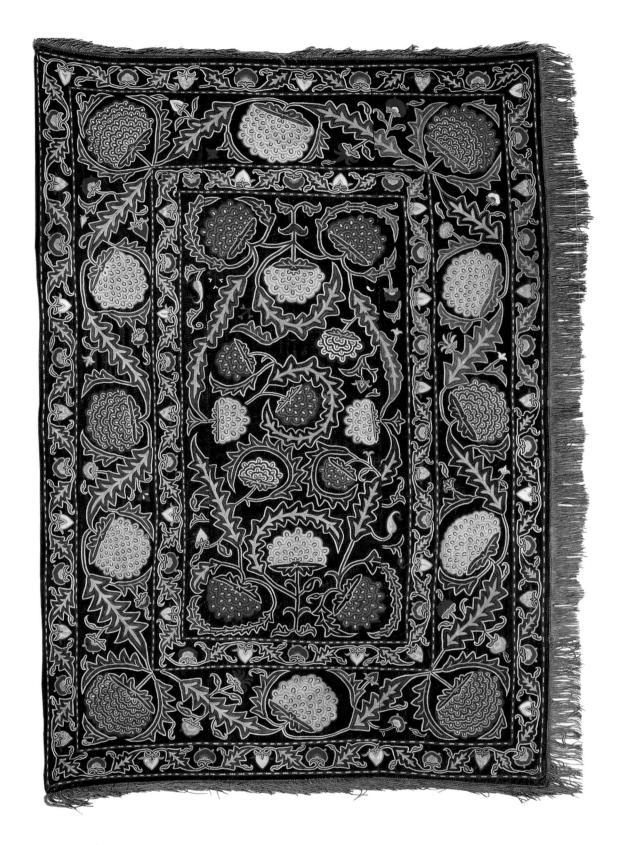

Nimsuzani (small wall hanging)
The principal motif on this small suzani is the seed-filled pomegranate (*anor nuska*), here shown cut open with its abundance of seeds in evidence. Symbols of fertility, pomegranates were also embroidered on clothing and skullcaps and the seeds were traditionally sprinkled onto a bride's skirt.
● Silk and wool *yurma* (chain stitch), tamboured on homespun silk fabric, silk fringe, made by Tajik or Uzbek women in the Bukhara region, Uzbekistan, late 1800s. 206 x 136 cm

Suzani (wall hanging)

A single large lozenge-shaped medallion covered with embroidery characterises a small, spectacular group of suzanis made only in Bukhara in the second half of the 1800s. Emanating rays strongly suggest the sun. Remnants of ancient sun worship still survive in Central Asia where images of the sun are thought to protect people from harm.

● Silk and wool *basma* (couching) on *karbos* (hand-woven cotton), vegetable dyes, made by Tajik or Uzbek women in Bukhara, Uzbekistan, 1850s. 288 x 188 cm

Nimsuzani (small wall hanging) ·

After about 1880, machine-woven coloured cottons imported from Russia were used as the base for embroidery. The circle, dominant in this design, is a powerful symbol of wholeness, protection and the union of opposites, of sun and moon, nature's cycles and meditation mandalas.

● Silk *yurma* (chain stitch) on machine-woven cotton, made by Tajik or Uzbek women, possibly in Gizduvan near Bukhara, Uzbekistan, late 1800s. 198 x 117 cm

Chapan (man's coat)
Robes like this one, laden with elaborate gold embroidery, enjoyed wide significance as ceremonial gifts in Central Asia. Ritual exchanges of gold embroidered robes and other items between the Amir and his courtiers and administrators were a regular event in Bukhara. These robes were also commonly presented as diplomatic gifts, a practice which endures to the present day.
● Gold thread embroidery (*zarduzi*) on silk velvet, silk ikat lining, made in Bukhara, Uzbekistan, late 1800s. 145 x 83 cm

Chapan (man's coat)

Fabulous gold embroidered coats like this were produced by professional male embroiderers in the Amir's workhop in Bukhara. By the late 1800s, as many as 25 private professional workshops were also operating in the city. These catered to the needs of prosperous Bukhara citizens as well as the Amir and his courtiers.

● Gold thread embroidery (*zarduzi*) on silk velvet, silk ikat lining, made in Bukhara, Uzbekistan, late 1800s. 148 x 85 cm

BRIGHT FLOWERS

Chapan (man's coat)
Gold embroidery played a special role in Bukhara society as an expression of meaning in both public and private life. Wearers were required to observe a variety of stylistic and symbolic conventions determined by the Amir. Viewed as a highly sought-after embellishment on clothing, gold embroidery flourished as a luxury market commodity.
● Gold thread embroidery (*zarduzi*) on silk velvet, silk ikat lining, made in Bukhara, Uzbekistan, late 1800s. 147 x 83cm

Salla (turban)

Men's headgear typically consisted of a small cap to absorb sweat underneath an embroidered cap, around which the turban cloth was wrapped. While most turbans were plain or striped, those worn at court were ornamented with gold embroidery. This example was among the confiscated property of the Amir of Bukhara.

● *Zarduzi-gulduzi-zaminduzi* (gold thread embroidery) on cotton muslin, made in the Bukhara region, Uzbekistan, late 1800s. 75 x 642 cm (unwrapped)

BUKHARA STATE ART AND ARCHITECTURAL MUSEUM, UZBEKISTAN, KP 1761/9. PHOTO BY KONSTANTIN MINAYCHENKO

Menseacha (child's boots)

In a society founded on mounted nomadism, children began to learn to ride at three or four years of age. When these boots were made for a privileged child, only a small percentage of Turkestan was occupied by the agricultural oasis culture of the towns and villages.

● *Zarduzi* (gold embroidery) on velvet, made in a professional workshop in Bukhara, Uzbekistan, late 1800s.

BUKHARA STATE ART AND ARCHITECTURAL MUSEUM, UZBEKISTAN, KP1 674/9. PHOTO BY KONSTANTIN MINAYCHENKO

Joinamaz (prayer mat)

The *joinamaz* was an important component of the dowry a young bride brought to her new husband's home. Praying towards Mecca five times a day is a vital Islamic religious practice. The embroidery on this example harmonises beautifully with the tie-dyed ikat ground cloth.

● Silk and wool *yurma* (chain stitch) on *adras* (ribbed silk and cotton fabric) ikat, vegetable dyes, made by Tajik or Uzbek women in the Bukhara region, Uzbekistan, mid 1800s. 137 x 87 cm

Suzani (wall hanging)
Although suzani designs vary across the production area in western Turkestan, certain patterns recur. The eight-pointed star form containing a large central rosette is found around Bukhara and Nurata as well as the Tashkent and Pskent regions. Identifiable irises appear between the stylised rosettes.
● Silk *yurma* (chain stitch) on ochre *karbos* (hand-woven cotton), vegetable dyes, made by Tajik or Uzbek women in the Bukhara region, Uzbekistan, late 1800s. 253 x 148 cm

Suzani (wall hanging)

The influence of Indian and Turkish embroidery is evident in this suzani. Lily-of-the-valley sprigs curl at the tip in the manner of Mughal art and in the centre is a *boteh* motif, common in Indian textiles and known as the *bodum* (almond) in Central Asia. Carnations reminiscent of those in Ottoman embroidery can be seen in the border. Two tiny vessels symbolise water.

● Silk *basma* (couching) and *yurma* (chain stitch) on *karbos* (hand-woven cotton), made by a Tajik or Uzbek woman in the Nurata region, Uzbekistan, mid 1800s. 258 x 160 cm

Suzani (wall hanging)
Characteristic of Nurata suzanis is the relatively naturalistic rendering of the flowers. In the central field of this suzani various different flowers are set within a grid formed by large, diagonally set leaves. The border, typically for Nurata suzanis, is about a quarter the width of the field.
● Silk *basma* (couching) and *yurma* (chain stitch) on *karbos* (handwoven cotton), vegetable dyes, made by Tajik or Uzbek women in the Nurata region, Uzbekistan, mid 1800s. 230 x 170 cm

Suzani (wall hanging)

Although small, Nurata was a provincial centre for trade between Kazakhstan and the cities of the Bukhara Emirate. This probably stimulated commercial as well as domestic production of suzanis, which were widely dispersed via the trade routes, resulting in a surprising number of surviving suzanis in naturalistic Nurata style.

● Silk *basma* (couching stitch) and *yurma* (chain stitch) embroidery on *karbos* (hand-woven cotton), made by Tajik or Uzbek women in the Nurata region, Uzbekistan, mid 1800s. 233.5 x 169 cm

Suzani (wall hanging)
A motif known as *chor chirog*, meaning 'four-wicked lamp', appears in both the centre and borders of this suzani. The protective nature of fire and its centrality to ritual is well entrenched in Central Asia. For example, a lighted lamp was borne around the heads of a bride and groom at their wedding.
● Silk and wool *basma* (couching) and *yurma* (chain stitch) on hand-woven cotton (*karbos*), made by Tajik or Uzbek women in the Samarkand region, Uzbekistan, mid 1800s. 222 x 161 cm

Suzani (wall hanging)
Each of the roundels on this suzani from Samarkand contains an eight-petalled flower with a rosette at the centre. Closer inspection reveals sharp points within the petals, identified as the *tegcha* (chisel) motif. This is believed to have a protective function, fending off danger from all directions.
● Silk *basma* (couching) and *yurma* (chain stitch) on machine-woven cotton, vegetable dyes, made by Tajik or Uzbek women in the Samarkand region, Uzbekistan, 1880–1890. 285 x 190 cm
SAMARKAND STATE MUSEUM OF HISTORY AND ARCHITECTURE, UZBEKISTAN, KP625 153-93. PHOTO BY KONSTANTIN MINAYCHENKO

Ruijo (wedding-bed sheet)

This bright mid twentieth-century *ruijo* illustrates the continuity of fine domestic embroidery during the Soviet era in Uzbekistan. The large spiralling motifs in the border may be interpreted as water wheels, commonly seen in the oases, or as cosmic symbols, representing the turning of the universe. ● Silk *yurma* (chain stitch) on glazed cotton and synthetic ground cloth, made by Tajik or Uzbek women in the Nurata region, Uzbekistan, about 1950. 240 x 187 cm

STATE MUSEUM OF APPLIED ARTS, TASHKENT, UZBEKISTAN, KP7061 1033-XX. PHOTO BY KONSTANTIN MINAYCHENKO

Joinamaz (prayer mat)

The entire ground of this prayer mat is covered with *iroqi* embroidery, or half cross stitch, a type of counted thread embroidery. Unlike free-form *yurma* and *basma* embroidery, designs tend to follow a grid. *iroqi* is only worked by settled women in Shakhrisabz and nearby Kitab.
● Silk *iroqi* (half cross stitch) on cotton, *adras* (fine silk warp with thick cotton weft) lining, made by Tajik or Uzbek women in the Shakhrisabz region, Uzbekistan, late 1800s. 194 x 183 cm

Suzani (wall hanging)

The design of this flamboyant suzani is deceptively simple. Nine strong roundels are evenly distributed with a *bodum* (almond) motif in each corner of the central field, and flowers and leafy tendrils filling the spaces between. It is brought alive by the masterful choice of complementary and contrasting colours.

● Silk *yurma* (chain stitch) on silk, printed cotton lining, made by Tajik or Uzbek women in Kitab, near Shakhrisabz, Uzbekistan, 1900–1910. 235 x 216 cm

BRIGHT FLOWERS

Suzani (wall hanging)
Bright flowers of pomegranates sprout from the slender stems of a single central plant, with curling leaf sprays and blooms filling the spaces between. The border of palmette motifs is a perfect complement. Contrasting colours in close tones are often favoured in suzanis from Shakhrisabz, with chain stitch (*yurma*) outlines in complementary shades.
● Silk *yurma* (chain stitch), tamboured on brown cotton twill, made by Tajik or Uzbek women in the Shakhrisabz region, Uzbekistan, late 1800s. 235.5 x 169 cm
BUKHARA STATE ART AND ARCHITECTURAL MUSEUM, UZBEKISTAN, KP12 1821/10 PHOTO BY KONSTANTIN MINAYCHENKO

Dauri (horse blanket)

On festive occasions, urban Central Asian men decked their horses in large ornamental blankets (*dauri*). The blanket was usually lined with a beautiful fabric, which was revealed when the rider tucked it back during bursts of speed. Back and sides are nearly always fringed with silk.

● Silk *iroqi* (half cross stitch) on cotton, fringed velvet border and *adras* lining, worked by Tajik or Uzbek women in the Shakhrisabz region, Uzbekistan, late 1800s. Length: 149 cm

BUKHARA STATE ART AND ARCHITECTURAL MUSEUM, UZBEKISTAN, KP1 1030/10. PHOTO BY KONSTANTIN MINAYCHENKO

Kurta (woman's dress)
Adras, from which this special-occasion *kurta* was made, is a finely ribbed cloth woven with a heavy cotton weft on closely set silk warps. The main motif is again the circle, ornamented with an unusual chequerboard design. The flower motifs on the cuffs are strongly reminiscent of ancient stone carvings from the region.
● Silk *basma* (couching) on *adras* (ribbed silk and cotton fabric), applied sequins, worked by a Tajik woman in the Bukhara region, Uzbekistan, early 1900s. 113 x 172 cm

SAMARKAND STATE MUSEUM OF HISTORY AND ARCHITECTURE, UZBEKISTAN, KP324 E13–7. PHOTO BY KONSTANTIN MINAYCHENKO

Ruband (face veil)
Face veils, such as this one for a wedding, are made by mountain Tajik women in the area around Dushanbe, and are only worn in the regions of Garm and Darvas. They feature archaic geometric embroidery and are tied around a bride's head under a shawl to cover her face and upper body before going to her husband's house.
● Silk satin stitch on cotton, made in the Darvas region of Tajikistan, early 1900s. 70 x 60 cm

Kurtai chakan (woman's dress)
Women of the Kulyab region once embroidered only small breast pieces and narrow sleeve bands for their dresses. From around 1900, embroidery gained in popularity and women began to cover the entire front and deep sleeve bands of their festive dresses with bright floral embroidery.
● Silk stem-stitch embroidery on cotton, made by a Tajik woman in the Kulyab region, Tajikistan, early 1900s. Height 130 cm

MUSEUM OF ETHNOGRAPHY, DUSHANBE, TAJIKISTAN, DME 15 (306-387) (VEIL); KP 9-56 (DRESS). PHOTOS BY GENNADY RATUSHENKO

Suzani (wall hanging)
Worked with a very delicate touch, this suzani features a large central medallion and quarter medallions in the corners. It is thus similar in design to many pile weave carpets. The cotton ground cloth was probably imported from Russia, although the Hissar region was known for its weavers.
● Silk *yurma* (chain stitch) on machine-woven glazed cotton, made by Tajik women in Karatag village, near Hissar, Tajikistan, about 1920s. 220 x 170 cm

Suzani (wall hanging)
Ura Tube in northern Tajikistan is a leading centre of embroidery. This suzani belongs to a design group in which the surface is covered with densely packed red flowers. The flowers are encircled with brown and very dark blue leaves and grow in the same direction.
● Silk *basma* (couching) and *ilmok* (chain stitch variant) on *karbos* (handwoven cotton), made by Tajik women in the Ura Tube region, Tajikistan, late 1800s. 240 x 182 cm
MUSEUM OF ETHNOGRAPHY, DUSHANBE, TAJIKISTAN, 369. PHOTO BY GENNADY RATUSHENKO

Suzani (wall hanging)
Balancing the strength of the large central roundel-in-an-eight-pointed-star motif are rows of smaller roundels, rosettes and palmettes. Those in the border may however be identified as pomegranates. Surrounding these strong circular forms and adding lightness is a mass of delicately drawn flowers and leaves.
● Silk *basma* (couching) and *ilmok* (chain stitch variant) on *karbos* (hand-woven cotton), made by Tajik women in the Khudjand region, Tajikistan, early 1900s. 300 x 185 cm

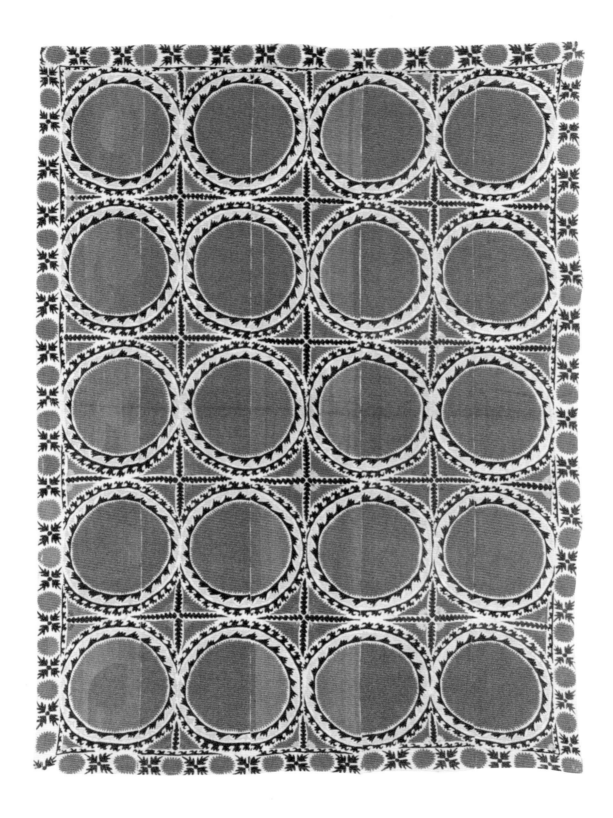

Oi palyak (moon wall hanging)
Characteristic of large embroidered dowry textiles from around Tashkent and nearby Pskent are spectacular moon (*oi*) and star (*yulduz*) motifs. The worship of astrological bodies was integral to the religious practices of the ancient agricultural population of the region. Tashkent is one of the oldest towns in Central Asia.
● Silk *basma* (couching) on *karbos* (handwoven cotton), made by Tajik or Uzbek women in the Tashkent region, Uzbekistan, late 1800s. 245 x 180 cm

Suzani (wall hanging)

In contrast to the plain exterior of a Central Asian house, the interior was preferably a riot of colour and pattern. Suzanis were complemented by soft carpets, wall paintings, intricately carved and painted ceilings, glazed ceramic platters, decorative metalware stacked in wall niches, and bright robes and embroidered caps that were hung around.

● Silk *basma* (couching) and *yurma* (chain stitch) on *karbos* (handwoven cotton), made by Tajik or Uzbek women in the Tashkent region, Uzbekistan, mid 1800s. 220 x 189 cm

Olti oilik palyak (six moon wall hanging)

The name given to embroideries from around Tashkent is *palyak*, from the Arabic word for firmament, or the heavens. The number of moons on a *palyak* varies from six to 40. In general, the fewer the moons, the more recent the embroidery.

● Silk *basma* (couching) and *yurma* (chain stitch) on cotton, made by Tajik or Uzbek women in the Tashkent region, Uzbekistan, late 1800s to early 1900s. 260 x 215 cm

Yulduz palyak (star wall hanging)
Suzanis from Pskent can generally be distinguished from those made in Tashkent by the division of the field into large hexagons and squares. *Yulduz* (star) motifs predominate, while the palette in both towns is principally red, yellow and black.
● Silk and cotton *basma* (couching) and *ilmok* (chain stitch variant) on cotton, made by Tajik or Uzbek women in the Pskent region, Uzbekistan, late 1800s.
263 x 216 cm

Palyak (wall hanging)
Typical of *palyak* from Pskent, the entire surface is covered with *basma* (couching) and the design is organised by simple geometry. Each rectangular compartment is intricately and variously ornamented with circles, flowers, stars and leaves.
● Silk *basma* (couching) embroidery on cotton, made by Tajik or Uzbek women in the Pskent region, Uzbekistan, late 1800s. 264 x 204 cm

Koylek (wedding dress) and **kamzol** (coat)
During Kazakh wedding rituals, the bride's richly embroidered velvet garments were hidden from view by a fine white net falling from an elaborate conical hat. The headwear and jewellery worn by both bride and groom were prepared long before the wedding.
● Gold embroidery on silk velvet, made in Kazakhstan, early 1900s. Height: 140cm (dress), 90cm (coat).

Kimishek (married woman's headdress)
According to Kazakh tradition, a married woman should conceal her most alluring features from everyone but her husband. The white cotton *kimishek*, worn under a kerchief or turban, covered her head and shoulders and was also known as *kyieli kyim* (sacred cloth).
● Silk half chain stitch embroidery with glass beads and sequins on cotton, made by a Kazakh woman in Taldi Kurgan Oblast, Kazakhstan, early 1900s, 81 x 132 cm

Sandik kap (cover for dowry chest)
The dowry chest was often placed in front of the *tuskiz* in the yurt, piled high with folded colourful quilts and pillows. An embroidered cover protected the chest from damage during the family's nomadic wanderings.
● Silk embroidery on sateen, wool felt, made by Mrs D Tinibaeva in Kazakhstan, 1950. 34 x 68 cm

Tuskiz (tent hanging)

The *tuskiz* was hung in the yurt (felt tent), embellishing it and creating an illusion of space. Important guests would be seated in front, framed by the border. The host's wealth and status were reflected in the embroidery, which was considered a talisman to bring good fortune.

● Chain and stem stitch, cotton, silk velvet, otter fur, made by an older woman for her own yurt in central Kazakhstan, late 1800s. 160 x 280 cm

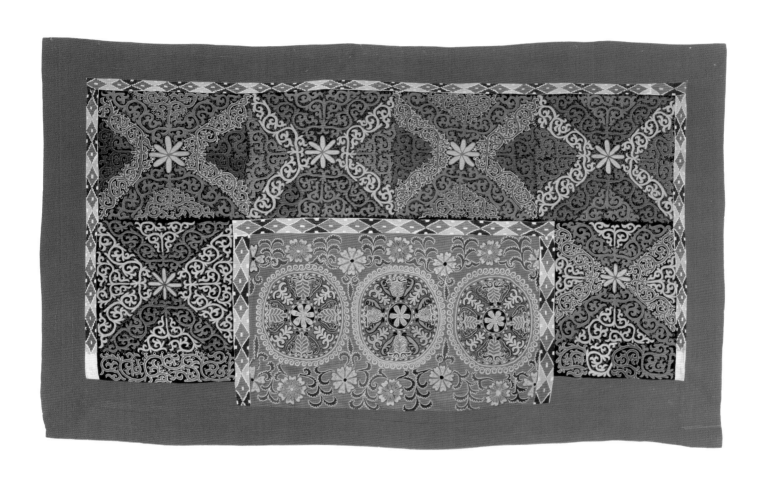

Tuskiz

A Kazakh bride would bring a *tuskiz* with her to her husband's yurt as part of her dowry. The quality of the embroidery reflected her skills and consequently her value as a wife. Most motifs were stitched in two colours. Warm colours were traditionally preferred.

● Cotton embroidery on silk velvet, made in eastern Kazakhstan, early 1900s. 137 x 242 cm

Borik (man's hat)
Wolves and foxes were a serious threat to the nomads' flocks of sheep. Their fur, made into garments, provided essential protection from the harsh winters of the Kazakh steppes. This hat, with its opulent fox fur trim, would have been worn by a wealthy older man under a larger brimmed hat.
● Padded gold embroidery and beads on silk velvet, fox fur trim, made in western Kazakhstan, late 1800s.

Ayir-kalpak (man's broad-brimmed hat)
Gold embroidery was usually worked by men as a woman's hands were believed to tarnish the gold threads. This wide-brimmed hat would have been worn by a man of status with the brims overlapping at the side.
● Gold embroidery on silk velvet, made in north Kazakhstan, late 1800s. Height: 49 cm

Flowers of the kiln

ceramics

Guy Petherbridge

IT IS LATE SPRING in 2004 in the upper Sukhandarya valley in southern Uzbekistan, adjacent to Tajikistan. Stark peaks, still crested with gleaming snow, form a backdrop to the provincial market town of Denau in the flat river plain. At this time of the year the lower slopes of the encircling ranges are quickly becoming carpeted in bright green alpine grasses, bejewelled with vermilion-red tulips. Denau lies on the ancient trade route linking Kashgar in western China with the Sukhandarya through the Kyzyl Suu valley which slices through the mountain massifs of Tajikistan.

It is Saturday, market day. Master potter, Mukhammad Rasul Zukhurov, bearded and comfortable in his flowing grey *chapan* (robe) in the crisp spring sun, sits quietly at his stall, as he does most market days. This area of town teems with people, selling and buying fruit and vegetables, baskets for the flat round *tandir*–(clay oven) baked Uzbek bread (*non*), fodder, animals, textiles and sewing materials, metal and plastic wares and tools. The market is full of the sound of motorbikes, cars and buses and the heroic, romantic Uzbek popular music played by tape sellers. The black caps (*doppe*) of Uzbek men, with their schematic white chilli pepper designs, punctuate the crowd. Occasionally a turbaned old man and his wife, her head and shoulders shrouded in her long embroidered *paranja* (veiling cloak, long hidden away from the Soviet confiscations of the late 1930s until they came out of the closet into the post-independence Islamic sun), can be seen shopping amongst the crowd. Electric-blue velvet *chapans* of both young and old men form a periodic visual counterpoint.

Yusuf Hasanov, a shepherd and small land-holder from a village some 15 kilometres from Denau, has come by horse to buy tools, seeds, spices and rice. A torrid, panting furnace of a summer fast approaches in this part of Uzbekistan. There is electricity in Yusuf's small village but, like most families, his has no refrigerator. Water—a true staple of all life in this land—is customarily kept cool for drinking in porous earthenware jugs and ewers with a fresh pine cone as an aromatic stopper.

Last week one of Yusuf's brother's children broke the spout of the ewer he had bought two decades ago from Usto (Master) Zukhurov's brother, a potter who has since died. There were a number of potters working in Denau then. At that time, Yusuf also bought a set of large ceramic *lagans* from the potter for his wedding party to serve the traditional *plov*—the rich communally shared, heaped rice, mutton, yellow carrot, onion and cumin dish—without which no feast or hosting of a guest is complete across Central Asia. The form, design and technology of these large dishes follow antecedents dating back to between the eighth and tenth centuries in the Middle East and the spread of Islam into Middle Asia—perpetuated until present day by the potters of Denau and Urgut, near Samarkand to the north-west.

The villagers around Denau know that Usto Zukhurov always has some of his little squat earthenware water jugs and ewers for sale at his stall, alongside other simple practical earthenware and copper-green glazed pottery items which both town and village people need and want.

Yusuf's son, Ulugbek, has a new baby and his wife, Guzal, has asked him to buy a *tuvak* for the traditional brightly painted wooden cradle. The *tuvak* is a little cylindrical earthenware peepot, glazed in the interior and with a broad circular lip, placed under the swaddled baby in the cradle—the nappy of Islamic Middle Asia. Each surviving traditional working potter in Central Asia still has a good business making *tuvaks*, often hundreds or more a year being produced in each workshop.

Usto Zukhurov embodies both the challenges and the hopes inherent in the situation of the old craft masters in Central Asia. He is rightly proud of the official acknowledgment, awards and support accorded him by the Soviet Union and independent Uzbekistan but he has learnt that ways of life, expectations and markets are subject to change and it is not easy for potters to make enough to live on now. Zukhurov, and the craft he represents and perpetuates, still plays a minor but integral role in Sukhandaryan society. Life in the big cities is changing due largely to the transition from a socialist central command to global market economies. In this conservative traditional region, with its relative poverty and reliance on local resources, the modern market economies are having a slower effect.

Master potter Mukhammad Rasul Zukhurov of Denau in Sukhandarya at his wheel, trimming the base of a bowl after it has been thrown and left to dry leather-hard.
PHOTO BY SVETLANA OSIPOVA, 2003

Previous page: detail of ceramic platter (see page 125)

The case of the Denau pottery tradition and Usto Zukhurov exemplifies what is happening in Uzbekistan and the potential for what could happen elsewhere in the region. In 2002 the Uzbekistan office of the Swiss Agency for Cooperation and Development initiated a program of support for Zukhurov and his tradition, headed by Svetlana Osipova. With the Denau master, the Uzbek-Swiss team have worked to revitalise the local pottery manufacture, restoring the workshop, aiding in the training of apprentices and encouraging the revival of decorative forms no longer saleable locally.

They have supported the building of a new wood-fired kiln after many years of gas being used as a fuel, and are working to educate the public of the significance and attraction of the ceramic works of Denau.

Usto Zukhurov is once again producing the full range of his ancestral ceramics, including the bright, impressionist, cobalt blue, antimony yellow and copper green on white flowered *lagans* (platters). All Central Asian potters producing glazed wares decorate many of their dishes, bowls and other vessels with vibrant, bright flowers and vegetal motifs. These often mirror or complement the designs and colours of the embroidered, woven and printed textiles which bring warmth, brightness and tradition to festive occasions and the interiors of homes across the region.

Across the 1200 years or more of Islamic culture in Central Asia, the region has been a participant in a much broader cultural zone in which many material culture traits and technologies were shared, including those of the potter and the potter's wares. Although in recent times, and indeed since the late 1600s and 1700s, the region has not played a politically or culturally dominant role in relation to neighbouring regions, this was not the case for much of the history of Islam. Dynasties of Central Asian origin— including the Samanids in the ninth century, the Seljuks in the tenth and eleventh centuries, the Timurids in the 1300s and 1400s and the Shaibanids in the 1500s—controlled vast expanses of the Islamic world to the south and west. Potters and their products often moved considerable distances through this pan-Islamic world and techniques, designs and aesthetic preferences (and expectations of their customers) were often shared. The survival and sustainability of Central

The Chor Minor Madrasa, Bukhara, Uzbekistan built in the mid 1800s. The tops of the minarets are covered in multi-coloured mosaic tiles and capped with turquoise tiles — a characteristic example of Central Asian potters' art applied to the fired clay or dried earth of the building.
PHOTO BY GUY PETHERBRIDGE, 2002

Asian ceramic traditions are thus of interest and importance not only to the individual crafts producers and others in the region itself but also internationally as a unique living testament to mainstream Islamic ceramic and cultural history.

The wares produced and used throughout this vast region still have not taken their proper place in the history of Islamic ceramics and in the collections visible to the world's public. The survival of these ceramic traditions in Central Asia and the wealth of excavated artifacts provide important revelations about the practices of Islamic pottery production, its role in society and precious material for ethno-archaeological research. Although the first publications on the subject appeared in Russia in the late 1800s and archaeologists and art historians have contributed substantially to the ceramic history of that time, only recently is a satisfactorily comprehensive history being assembled through the ongoing efforts of archaeologists and other researchers from Central Asia and elsewhere.

A brief history of Central Asian ceramics

Fired clay has long been a fundamental component of the material culture of the peoples of Central Asia. Since at least the sixth millennium BCE the abundant clays and minerals of the region have been used to fashion a diversity of practical and ritual items. The extensive archaeological and other investigations carried out across the region for over 100 years have revealed a great wealth and variety of ceramic wares and forms, some of extreme technical and morphological subtlety and sophistication, particularly amongst the early and later urbanised civilisations of the region.

For millennia, the pottery across this vast terrain, while diverse in form and function, was basically simple earthenware, selected and fired at relatively low temperatures. In earlier times it was handbuilt or coiled and was fired in the open air—techniques used to the present day in more remote mountain areas without a substantial settled population such as Badakhshan in the high Pamirs of south-east Tajikistan and northern Afghanistan. Hand moulding, coiling and paddle-beating was the predominant way of forming pots. In recent times for which we have records, women were the main potters of handbuilt pieces, producing for their families and neighbourhood. The wares were sometimes highly burnished and were often decorated in geometric patterns of long ancestry, reflecting in many ways the patterns of cross-stitched embroidered textiles, carpets and flatweaves of these areas. Later, in urbanised areas, the potter's wheel was introduced and updraught kilns of varying configuration were used.

Decoration, if applied, was incised, appliquéd, moulded, drawn or painted using solutions of suspensions of ground red and ochre-coloured oxides and other minerals. It was only with the introduction of Islam in the ninth and tenth centuries CE and the technologies accompanying it, that the potters of Central Asia began to use ceramic glazes. The Parthian and Sassanian cultures on the

A 1930s photograph of a family of women potters working in the Faisabad region of Tajikistan—one of the last areas in Central Asia to preserve the ancient traditions of hand-forming earthenware.

PHOTO FROM THE KAMOLEDDIN BEZHOD NATIONAL MUSEUM OF TAJIKISTAN

Master potter Bakhtiyor Sattorov of Kasbi, Kashkadarya. Usto Sattorov is one of the few Central Asian potters following the ancient traditions of wheel-formed, kiln-fired, unglazed earthenware.

PHOTO BY GUY PETHERBRIDGE, 2001

southern fringes of this area did however use monochrome lead and alkaline glazes, and early glass makers in Central Asia were familiar with the materials and technologies used for alkaline ceramic glazes, which were to become key to the potters of the region.

Some earthenware pottery has shown remarkable historical continuity throughout much of Central Asia, changing little over time. The production of low-temperature ware was a fundamentally efficient process. Low firing temperatures and short firing times limited the amount of fuel required—important in dry areas where surplus vegetation was not to be wasted and fuel often had to be painstakingly gathered and carted from a distance.

In the extremely hot, dry summers characteristic of Central Asia, porous earthenware kept water and liquid milk products cool through transpiration and evaporation. In the remote village of Kasbi in the Kashkadarya steppes of southern Uzbekistan, earthenware ewers, jars and churns of a hard-fired, fine, light-toned clay are still produced. The water ewers, jugs and drinking pitchers produced here today are practically indistinguishable in body and form from artifacts excavated across a broad geographical and temporal expanse from Nishapur to Samarkand to Turkestan and from the Middle Ages to the 1800s. Similarly Kasbi storage jars have forms and applied decoration characteristic of artifacts of three and four millennia ago.

In the social philosophy of Islam as practised in Middle Asia, the provision of water to the passer-by was a meritorious act. Households would place a large porous water jar on a stand in the street outside for the passing traveller or neighbour—somewhere shady and preferably where the pots would be further cooled by a breeze. In some regions, such as the Ferghana Valley in eastern Uzbekistan, householders would keep a frog in the water jar as an indicator of purity in the belief that frogs do not live in impure water. Honoured guests would be welcomed and water poured over their hands in an act of purification from an ornamented ewer.

Another often overlooked traditional use of earthenware is that of the humble flowerpot. An artifact made by every workshop, it is often an economical mainstay of the Central Asian potter if times are lean. Central Asian peoples love flowers and they are grown everywhere; in pots lining the tiny balconies of the Soviet high-rises of towns and cities and the larger collective rural settlements and saturating with colour the courtyards of the Uzbeks and Tajiks and the north and eastern Turkmen. Exquisitely tended by the women of the extended household, these gardens are rich and fragrant with fruit-bearing trees, shady grape-covered trellises, and pots and beds of assorted herbs and flowers.

Master potter Mirzabakhrom Abduvakhobov of the Ferghana Valley, Uzbekistan produces ceramic ware vibrantly decorated in flowers and plant motifs, evoking abundance and fertility.
PHOTO BY GUY PETHERBRIDGE, 1999

As water nourishes and cleanses the body, spirit and soul of the peoples of Central Asia, so does it nourish the soil and plants sustaining life. Water was traditionally moved from water source to canal, field and vegetable garden by waterwheels. Along the perimeter of the wheels were tied fired earthenware pots which scooped up water and emptied it into a sluice as the wheel revolved. These pots were required in great number and their manufacture was a basis for the livelihood of many pottery workshops. The traditional waterwheel became a source of inspiration for decoration amongst potters in the region, particularly for the large round *lagans*, dishes and bowls. In Andijon in the Ferghana Valley, for instance, its circular, spoked structure forms the basis for plate and bowl designs in glorious greens, yellows and blues and it is seen as a symbol of the ongoing water-fed cycles of seasons, abundance and life.

Long fundamental to Central Asian cooking is the *tandir*, a domed, clay slab-constructed earthenware oven of fundamentally the same construction across the region. Although electricity and gas became widely available across the Soviet Union, the *tandir* cooking of *somsas*, *pirogi*, *non* (flat Uzbek and Tajik bread), and the pine-resin-smoke flavoured roast meat dish, *archa gosht*, is such a strong tradition that this outdoor wood-fired oven has never been displaced by modern alternatives. So prevalent is the *tandir* today that potters who can no longer find the buyers, raw materials or fuel

Tandirs, the traditional hand-formed clay ovens of Central Asia, near Khiva, Khorezm, Uzbekistan. Still a valued essential for the cooking of traditional *somsas*, *pirogis* and roasted meat dishes, they are the most commonly produced clay artifact in Central Asia today.

PHOTO BY GUY PETHERBRIDGE, 2000

needed to make other types of pottery survive by making *tandir* ovens for local markets, and throughout Uzbekistan *tandir* makers still produce large quantities of these cooking ovens.

Archaeological records bear witness to the popularity of ceramic miniatures and toys in Central Asia. Excavated toy figurines and whistles dating from hundreds or thousands of years ago differ little in form and inspiration from those still made today, particularly for the traditional spring solstice celebration of Navroz, celebrated on 21 March. In the months prior, craftspeople (predominantly women) busy themselves producing fired clay and painted toys (*xushpaliak*) and whistles for sale in the local markets or large cities. Favourite subjects include birds, sheep, dogs, horses, fish, elephants, horses and riders, camels and mythological beings.

Glazing styles

Glazed ceramic technologies were adopted in Central Asia with the advance of Islamic culture from the south-west in the eigth to eleventh centuries CE. The range of ceramic glaze technologies introduced in the early centuries of Islam has continued to provide the basic technological repertoire of the region. The lead and alkaline glazes introduced both fluxed at a low temperature and the wares continued to be fired at low temperatures, meeting the fuel efficiencies, firing times and other requisites of the existing earthenware technologies which had proved so suitable for the region.

The most common traditional method of glaze decoration in the region is single-fired underglaze painting. In the underglaze technique the decoration is painted on the dry, unfired pot, which is then covered with a transparent glaze and fired. Double-firing and overglaze painting is also used for some glazed decoration, including tiles. Pottery may be decorated with earth slips (engobes), chemical glazes or by slip incising.

A fundamental feature of ceramic glazing technology in Central Asia, which formed the basis for much (probably most) ceramic production from the 1100s to the early 1900s was the use of alkaline glazes made from a pure silica sand or ground, fired quartz as the primary raw materials with plant ash as the flux. The plant ash (*ishkor*), high in sodium and potassium, enabled firing at relatively low temperatures (900–1000° C) and was obtained from a range of arid-environment plants. Usually these plants were harvested in the late summer or autumn from non-agricultural lands nearby, dried and then used as needed by the pottery workshops.

The *ishkor* ash was sieved and ground, then mixed with ground calcined white quartz (typically river pebbles) or pure sand and a little water, and formed into small balls or pellets which were then dried, kiln-fired and ground. This powder mixed with water formed the transparent overglaze and with ground quartz or sand frit (and sometimes an iron-free clay) was the key component of the slip, which was applied over a relatively porous earthenware or a stonepaste body. The result was a lustrous, soft-toned glaze complex in which the transparent glaze bonded well to a chemically and physically compatible slip ground.

The particular chemistry of an *ishkor* glaze affects the colours of chemicals used under it for decoration. The colours may differ, depending on the technique and glaze contents and according to whether an alkaline or lead glaze is used. For example, under an alkaline glaze, cobalt oxide produces a bright blue colour, copper oxide a light, rich turquoise blue, and manganese dioxide, brown. Under a transparent lead glaze, cobalt oxide produces a dark blue, copper oxide green, manganese dioxide, dark brown.

Lead glazes had been used in earlier times in Central Asia—indeed the earliest glazes in the area may have been monochrome lead glazes—but from the 1100s until the end of the 1800s, alkaline glazes had been the predominant glazes of Central Asian pottery. Lead glaze has now almost completely replaced alkaline glaze. The raw material is cheap, easy to use (it melts very easily), readily available in industrialised economies and is less labour-intensive to produce than alkaline glazes. Lead glazes permit a varied palette, including blues and greens as well as the reds, light yellows and oranges not possible using the traditional alkaline glaze materials of Central Asia. It is possible to modify the tonalities of blues and greens by using mixtures of lead and alkalis in a glaze.

Famous Uzbek toymaker, Khamro Rakhimova, of Uba near Bukhara, Uzbekistan shows her skills to a group of young village girls. Until her death some years ago, Rakhimova produced colourfully painted animal- and bird-shaped toys and whistles for the spring Navroz festival.

PHOTOGRAPHER UNKNOWN, 1960S

Although not a common feature of Central Asian ceramics, tin (stannic oxide) was used in glazes as an opacifier in early Islamic times. In subsequent centuries it was applied to some ceramics which were derivative of Chinese porcelain wares. It achieved a new localised popularity in the 1800s in some workshops in Samarkand, Tashkent and the Ferghana Valley. In Rishtan, it was used as an opaque, enamel-like glaze (*qalaili sir*) for *chinni* ware which imitated Qing period Chinese porcelain. Tin oxide is characteristically used with a much higher proportion of lead oxide.

Various kiln structures and internal configurations are traditional to Central Asia. A number from the Islamic period have been excavated by archaeologists in Merv (Turkmenistan), Otrar (Kazakhstan), Afrasiab (Uzbekistan) and other sites. The few surviving wood-fired kilns in present-day workshops are of the updraught type with a perforated kiln floor and a firebox below, although some examples from early Islamic times were fired in the same chamber as the ware. Until the early 1960s, when pottery was still a flourishing craft in Central Asia, most workshops, including the very large ones, fired with wood or related fuel materials. However, because of the low cost and availability of gas and electricity in the latter decades of the Soviet Union and immediate post-independence in the 1990s, most potters changed to one of these forms of energy, usually gas. Today gas supplies are not always reliable in some areas, particularly in winter, making it difficult for some potters to viably continue production.

The advent of colourful ceramic glazes technologies brought to the region a whole range of new decorative possibilities and new market expectations to the indigenous potters working there, setting in place the technological and design basis for what was to be over a millennium of subsequent potters.

The eighth to eleventh centuries CE in northern Iran, Khorasan, western Afghanistan and Transoxiania, the northern slopes and piedmonts of the ranges forming the border between Kazakhstan and Kyrgyzstan and the valleys of the Semireche region in south-eastern Kazakhstan saw the establishment and consolidation of Islam in a very particular way. This was a volatile period. In the absence of a strong, centralised religious administration, the flourishing communities and religious sects of the region developed a rich patchwork of local Islamic observances and traditions, which drew on the diversity of cultures and technologies preceding or introduced with the spread of Islam.

The Central Asian admiration for Chinese decorative arts is reflected in this tile mosaic at the entrance to the great Mir-i-Arab Madrasa in Bukhara, Uzbekistan, built in 1535–1536. It depicts a large Ming *meiping* style porcelain vase.

PHOTO BY GUY PETHERBRIDGE, 2003

The pottery-making complex of Usto Sattorov in Kasbi, Kashkadarya. Central Asian pottery masters often used a corner of their domestic courtyard (near the entrance) for their workshops. In the foreground are *tandirs* being made in the form characteristic of this locality.

PHOTO BY GUY PETHERBRIDGE, 2000

The heterogeneity of these communities, often living side by side in the major urban centres, is reflected in excavated glazed ceramics of the ninth to eleventh centuries CE in a great range of wares. Notwithstanding this diversity, certain distinct styles were shared across this broad region—styles once attributed to either Samarkand (Afrasiab) or Nishapur but which are likely to have been made in other places in Central Asia as well. In Tajikistan, recent excavations have revealed a local version of the epigraphic wares and in other locations in Kazakhstan, Uzbekistan and Tajikistan wares and designs not found elsewhere have been uncovered. These styles and technologies also influenced the wares of flourishing Christian, Manichaean and other minorities in the region. Ceramics produced for Christian and other communities have been identified as far east as Kyrgyzstan and Western China.

Islamic cultural developments in Iran continued to be an influencing factor in Central Asian ceramics, although the Shiite-Sunni divide lessened this impact from Safavid times on. Chinese arts and crafts also had an impact on ceramic design in Central Asia, often through the mediation of Chinese wares imported by sea into the Middle East and Iran or through the import of Islamic ceramics and other arts from other centres inspired by the Chinese. In the ninth to tenth centuries in Central Asia, splendid polychrome lead-glazed splash ware, evoking that of the Tang period, was produced in Afrasiab (modern-day Samarkand) and other centres.

By the 1100s the process of relative cultural homogeneity occurring in regional Islam is reflected in a less diverse range of wares which are generally distinctly local in character, although influences continued from the major ceramic centres of Iran. This period saw the increased uptake of alkaline glazed technologies, including the alkaline blue-glazed stonepaste or earthenware which was to become so popular across the region and across into China.

The social disruption of the Mongol invasions and their domination of vast areas is reflected in the ceramics of the period. The underlying regional ceramic technologies did not change although many new designs were introduced—very interesting and diverse ceramics have been excavated in various sites of this period, particularly in Kazakhstan. Mongol rule in China saw the introduction of blue and white porcelain in the 1300s. Catering to a Muslim market and exported to the Middle East, it became very popular and stimulated imitations which created strong new decorative trends in Islamic ceramic design which had their impact on Central Asia. A heightened influence from Chinese decorative arts occurred with the rise to power of Amir Timur in the late 1300s, bringing new imitations of Chinese designs and wares into the ceramic productions of Central Asia. These became a hallmark of the Timurids and the Shaibanids.

The decline in dominance of the Shaibanids in Central Asia in the late 1500s saw the consolidation of new power bases in the region through the khanates of Khiva, Bukhara and Kokand. While linked strongly by trade to their neighbours, these Uzbek states were powers only to themselves and not generators of major new decorative formulas. The ceramics in the region in the 1600–1700s saw a progressive regional adaptation of Timurid and Shaibanid designs. They also seem to have drawn to some degree on influences from the flourishing ceramic centres of eastern Iran and Khorasan (which were producing versions of blue and white ware of varying quality and sophistication) from where some exports would naturally have travelled north. Many centres produced their own stonepaste or faience wares in a very remotely derivative Chinese manner, alongside glazed and unglazed earthenware.

Women in Margilan in the Ferghana Valley, Uzbekistan preparing soup in the large metal cauldron, *kozon*, normally used for communal cooking. The bowl (*piala*) is the iconic food vessel of Central Asia, combining the functions of cup, bowl and dish.
PHOTO BY CHRISTINA SUMNER, 1999

Khorezm, to the north-west of the region, had always maintained a higher degree of independence in the face of competing regional powers. Its ceramics were less influenced by the schematised floral and naturalistic design developments of its neighbours and more by the geometric traditions of Islamic ceramics. In Khiva ceramic production surged strongly in the late 1800s, supporting the khan's active building campaigns. Tiles, decorated in a conservative Islamic geometric interlace manner, were produced in considerable volume and their design and technology is reflected to this day in the work of some Khorezm master potters.

Elsewhere in the region, some centres continued to follow and build on regional decorative traditions based on lead glazes, earth slip and chemical underglaze decoration. History records the movement of potters to other locations to work in the 1700s and 1800s, as had been the practice in previous times, resulting in a documented cross-fertilisation of techniques and designs between some of the major centres.

A new burst of ceramic inspiration occurred in the region with the Chinese takeover of Kashgar and other centres of the Tarim basin in the 1830s and the late 1800s and a new policy of opening borders with Central Asia promoting trade. Kashgar was an extension of Central Asian Islamic culture linked in many ways with the nearby Ferghana Valley and the Kokand khanate or dominion (which had dominated Kashgar from time to time in the 1700s and early 1800s). Potters from the Ferghana Valley trained in Kashgar during the late 1800s, and produced blue-and-white *chinni* stonepaste ware drawing strongly on Qing traditions. Rishtan, Kanibadam, Isfara and Chorku were major centres of this production. The last three, in modern-day northern Tajikistan, produced wondrous large platters—amongst the most beautiful in the history of world ceramics. In the 1900s Rishtan and neighbouring centres, serving the rural communities of the valley, such as Gurumsaray, produced more popular variations and adaptations of these designs in both *ishkor* and lead- and tin-glazed earthenware.

During the 1800s and early 1900s Central Asian potters continued to build on what had become strong local decorative traditions. Popular ceramics of the period drew particularly strongly on textile designs, just as textile designs drew inspiration and strength from ceramics—a natural occurrence in intimately linked communities which shared a use and knowledge of designs and their popular significance.

Tea vessel (*chaydish*),
Uzbekistan, late 1800s.
34.5 x 16 cm
GUY PETHERBRIDGE COLLECTION.
PHOTO BY GUY PETHERBRIDGE

The potters

Larger settled communities in Central Asia usually had a considerable number of potters (*kulols*), often living and working in their own neighbourhood or *mahalla*. Excavations at Otrar, a major city in southern Kazakhstan close to the Syr Darya River, have revealed just such quarters with numerous kilns and workshops. Potters' *mahallas* are recorded in Bukhara, Shakhrisabz, Samarkand and Tashkent. Rishtan, to this day is one of the principal centres of ceramic production in Uzbekistan and has long had a potters' *mahalla*. In the first decade of the 1900s it had 130 workshops, employing some 250 people. The only potters' *mahalla* which retains most of its original characteristics today is in the village of Uba close to Bukhara and Gizduvan. A number of potter families live in the same section of the village, producing dishes, vessels and clay toys, and they still share an ancient potters' mosque.

Today, possibly following an ancient practice, the workshops of potters in Central Asia are almost always located in their domestic complex or closely adjacent to it, often in a corner of the courtyard close to the entrance.

Potters in Central Asian urban societies were traditionally classed according to the broad category of pottery forms in which they specialised: *kosagarlik* (open vessels such as plates and dishes) or *kuzagarlik* (closed vessels such as ewers, jugs and jars). In some places potters were further classified according to the techniques in which they specialised; in Rishtan, for example, masters making high quality faience were called *chinnipaz*, those using white backgrounds and transparent alkali glazes, *okpaz*, and those using yellow lead glazes, *sariqpaz*.

An important ceramic craft in Islamic Central Asia was that of the tile maker. Tiles were an essential decoration for religious buildings, shrines, mausolea and tombs of any prestige, as they were for *caravanserai* and palaces. They were also used in decorating homes in some of the old cities (in some homes in Chorsu, the old centre of Tashkent, Uzbekistan, for example, a number of courtyards had decorated tiled features). Tiles are becoming a new mainstay of a number of potters as government restoration programs draw on their traditional skills. New public buildings use tile facings and (as is the case in Khiva and Bukhara) hotels and restaurants servicing the growing tourism industry draw on local traditional crafts and designs to decorate their establishments.

Most ceramics were sold from the workshop or the local market. Demand was generally stable in a society which relied on a broad range of domestic, constructional and agricultural ceramic wares, unless there was competition from imported wares. Even then potters tended to be responsive to their local communities, their needs and changing fashions, often producing more affordable imitations of imported ware. Thus many centres, particularly those in the Ferghana Valley produced copies of Chinese porcelain. These more expensive *chinni* wares, produced in centres such as Rishtan, were of a stonepaste body which attempted to imitate the porcelain itself, while more rural potters produced even more distant and cheaper imitations of blue, green and white *ishkor* glazes on a earthenware body. Some potters like those of Kanibadam, Isfara and Chorku sold to a broad and distant market (until competition from Tashkent put an end to this).

With the establishment of a Soviet administration in Central Asia in the early 1920s, the Soviet government declared its concern for craftspeople. In practice, however, the government worked towards the conversion of craftspeople to factory workers and the ultimate elimination of craftsmen as a class. But state ideology and human realities often proved incompatible and compromises were reached. The new administration managed local traditional industries through the formation of ceramic works and cooperatives which supplied all the ceramic needs of society. These artels and other cooperative associations existed until the 1960s. They relied mainly on traditional technologies, although new machinery was introduced to facilitate some of the heavier work.

Master potter, Samad Asadov, of Uba, near Bukhara, Uzbekistan with his grandsons outside the workshop door in their domestic courtyard. Central Asian master potters customarily passed their skills onto the young boys of the family.
PHOTO BY GUY PETHERBRIDGE, 2004

The relative status quo changed in the 1950s and 1960s when the Soviet administration opened factories in the region which mass produced porcelain or other high-temperature ware versions of the bowls (*piala*) and teapots so iconic of Central Asian traditions. While the new factories provided increased employment in the ceramic industry and boosted production, these industrial innovations had a major negative impact on the traditional hand pottery producers. To counter this impact, initiatives such as policies recognising the creative crafts and support of national artist craft masters were introduced.

Nevertheless, observers in the 1950s and 1960s still commented on the abundance and vibrancy of folk ceramics sold in Central Asian markets. Potters did continue to work in some traditional centres producing vessels for which there was no acceptable alternative in industrial production, such as the large storage jars or *khums*, large earthenware water containers and special vessels for making and storing milk products, and the large decorated plates or *lagans*.

By the time the Soviet system collapsed in the early 1990s and the republics of Tajikistan, Turkmenistan, Kyrgyzstan, Kazakhstan and Uzbekistan gained independence, traditional pottery was being produced only in limited amounts and forms in Uzbekistan. Local factories and imports provided most ceramics needed in the home. Some centres of traditional ceramic manufacture, such as Kattakurgan and Jizzac in Uzbekistan, which had flourished only 25–30 years earlier had ceased pottery production for some time. In most cases where the craft survives only one or two pottery workshops are functioning in the town or village where once tens or hundreds worked.

The last traditional potter in Turkmenistan, Usto Sapaev, died in the second half of the 1990s. In Kazakhstan the traditional craft had died out by the time of independence, as had the traditions in Kyrgyzstan, although in both countries a small number of artist-potters work, trained in art schools and institutions in the Soviet Union. In Tajikistan, practitioners are restricted to a few masters working in the north in what is geographically and culturally a corner and part of the Ferghana Valley.

Thus by the late 1990s this region of such remarkable survival of venerable Islamic ceramic traditions was facing considerable challenges in a new global and market environment. Only in Islamic western China and Khiva and its environs in Khorezm, western Uzbekistan, is the traditional pottery craft flourishing with a number of workshops still producing considerable quantities of very low cost wares of traditional form, catering to the continuing demands of a local market and of the expanding neighbouring populations across the border in north east Turkmenistan.

Donyolbek Boltabaev and his Heritage Central Asia field survey team discuss local Khorezm wares with master potter Rajab Ortigov of Khiva and his son.
PHOTO BY GUY PETHERBRIDGE, 2000

Fortunately, in the post-independence Central Asia republics, the concern for the sustainability of the traditional trades and craftsmen extends beyond the preoccupations of the craftsmen themselves. Significant transitions in Central Asian societies have directed individuals with new energies to these matters. Small business entrepreneurs are taking an active interest. Government agencies are consciously building on cultural traditions in formulating new national identities. International bodies are concerned with the viability and potential productive contribution of handicrafts, and researchers are assisting traditional craft producers through international dialogue between specialists.

UNESCO's Intangible Heritage Section and its Tashkent Office are implementing the Blue of Samarkand Project, a major research, sustainability and publication program, providing practical support to a number of the surviving old master potters to help train a new generation of potters. The governments of Uzbekistan and Tajikistan are conscious and supportive of the needs of the surviving craftsmen. Tajikistan's ability to fund the needs however has been extremely limited following a difficult economic transition since the break-up of the Soviet Union and the ravages of a decade of civil war. In Uzbekistan, with its more thriving economy and greater numbers of high-profile surviving craftsmen, the government has initiated support for them through associations and heritage organisations such as Oltin Meros, through the introduction of a Living National Treasures system, and through UNESCO's collaboration with the Uzbek Ministry of Cultural Affairs. Heritage Central Asia, an international non-government organisation (NGO), is contributing to this work across the whole region.

The challenges to both the survival of the traditions and the livelihood of their practitioners and their families are being addressed in a number of ways. The task of sustaining the characteristics and viability of traditional crafts in very different market and social environments is no easier here than it is in other parts of the world. □

The Uzbek kulol

Akbar and Alisher Rakhimov

IN UZBEKISTAN, AS elsewhere in Central Asia, the potter or *kulol* played an essential role in traditional society. Ceramics not only had an important range of utilitarian functions, but also constituted an integral feature of domestic decoration and Uzbek social rituals. The rich diversity of pottery produced reflected its importance in everyday life. More than ten principle types of vessels were produced for household use, including some seven varieties of *tandirs* (ovens for bread baking) and *khums*, special containers for water and for storing foodstuffs. Craftsmen produced many small domestic items such as jars, lidded containers for salt storage (*tuzdon*), for bread (*nondon*), oil lamps (*chiroqdon*, *shamdon*) and whistles for children.

Ceramics were important in the many celebrations characteristic of Uzbek culture. For example, when a young woman married, her relatives would present her with various items of pottery, such as tea bowls (*pialas*), teapots (*chainiks*) and dishes. Families also used to purchase significant amounts of new pottery for the wedding feasts which occurred over a number of days with much food, music and many guests. Even today, local neighbourhood (*mahalla*) committees purchase pottery (*tuy lagans*, *pialas* and *chainiks*) for use by people living within the *mahalla* for wedding ceremonies and other neighbourhood and national festivities and receptions.

The *kulol* and his work had particularly valued symbolic and spiritual associations in Uzbek culture. History reveals that the famous ruler Amir Timur venerated a potter, Shamsiddin Kulol, as his *pir*—preceptor or holy spirit. The venerable Sufi Bahuddin Naqshbandi also has long been honoured in the region as a *pir* of craftsmen. Naqshbandi's *pir* was also a potter, Said Amir Kulol. Sufis have a traditional expression, 'with God in the soul—with hands in work'. Craftsmen customarily

started their works by asking the spirits of Bahuddin Naqshbandi and Shamsiddin to support their creations. There is a regional legend that the potter is connected with fire, and it was always considered that half the creation of a pot is the craftsman's work and half is through the magic of the fire. Therefore, the *kulol* felt the whole process of making pottery to be spiritually inspired and full of emotion.

AKBAR RAKHIMOV DECORATING A LARGE PLATTER IN HIS TASHKENT WORKSHOP.

FROM A A KHAKIMOV, *ATLAS OF CENTRAL ASIAN ARTISTIC CRAFTS AND TRADES, VOLUME I*, TASHKENT, 1999

Ceramic craftsmen are creators—and as such they also used to be excellent reciters of history and legend and masters of the popular performing arts. For instance, Usto (master) Hokim Satimov from Gurumsaray was both a master potter and a well-known singer and musician. When unloading completed works which he particularly liked from a kiln-firing, he would sing popular songs. Usto Satimov was much sought after

to perform during social events, particularly at weddings—it was a great pleasure for the master to play his *dutar* (traditional stringed musical instrument) and to sing for these local celebrations. Master *kulols* were also often renowned humorists. Drollery competitions often took place in the *chaihanas*, neighbourhood men's teahouses where craftsmen liked to get together after their working days to drink tea, cook *plov*, share news and discuss the issues of the day. Usto Abdullo Chinnipaz from the pottery centre of Rishtan was a widely appreciated drollery performer and comic.

The traditional ceramic craft was perpetuated through many successive generations within individual families— through entire dynasties of master potters. The craft was passed from grandfather, father or uncle to son or nephew—although occasionally craftsmen passed their skills to other relatives or neighbours. In order to attract children to the potter's craft, craftsmen started to teach them how to make small whistles when they were 6 to 8 years old. When the children saw how ordinary clay became transformed in this way, they became fascinated by this common material which is available to all. From the making of whistles, toys and miniatures, they then gradually moved towards the making of vessels.

The whistles were given the shape of roosters, horses, birds or dragons and were the product of each child's fantasy. During meetings craftsmen liked to show each other the first such works made by their young apprentices. If the masters saw successful creations, they would applaud and compliment them, saying that such an apprentice would have a good future as a potter. The craftsmen carefully selected talented and hardworking apprentices (*shogird*) with whom they shared their long experience and the secrets of their profession, so that they were able to continue

A GROUP PHOTO OF THE LEADING MASTER POTTERS OF
UZBEKISTAN MEETING UNDER THE AUSPICES OF THE
USTO ASSOCIATION IN ANDIJON, 1970s.

the traditions or school of the master. In this way apprentices became craftsmen. After being blessed by their master, and publicly and formally recognised by experienced craftsmen in their community, they could start to work independently as potters. Some potters now permit non-family members as apprentices, mainly because of the lack of interest of family members to follow the craft as they look to other occupations in a changing world.

Prior to the October Revolution of 1917, *kulols* and other craftsmen united into groups according to their professions. Each ceramic centre or corporation in the village, town or city used to have its own *aksakal* (head), selected by the potters as a body. These craftsmen's guilds were responsible for decision-making for all matters related to production and sale. It was also a long-standing custom in Uzbekistan and elsewhere in the Central Asian region for craftsmen to meet at each other's workshops to discuss newly created works. They would help colleagues with the supply of glaze and other materials and would exchange technologies. Craftsmen also went to other regions and learned from masters there, while maintaining the techniques and styles of their own regions.

In the 1920s, several years after the revolution, when people started establishing trade cooperatives, the Hunarmand Association was created in Rishtan, the Gonchar Association in Kattakurgan and the Birlik Association in Samarkand. In the 1930s, in order to gather all craftsmen under one body, an association called Kizil Kulol was formed where apprenticeship courses were also organised. In the same period in Samarkand associations were established which specialised in printing, embroidery and the production of musical instruments. After Tashkent was named as the capital of the Soviet Socialist Republic of Uzbekistan, a similar pottery cooperative

workshop association was opened in Tashkent, called the Baranov Artel. In 1960 this was renamed the Tashkent Ceramics Plant. In the same year ceramics plants were established in Rishtan, Andijan, Khorezm and Kitab under the Ministry of Local Industry. Many traditional pottery masters were obliged to work in such industrialised ceramics plants which were devoted entirely to mass production. By the 1980s unnecessary products filled the state warehouses, and the *kulols* who worked at those plants lost their traditional hand-manufacturing skills and styles and their dignity as national masters.

In the 1970s several Uzbek master potters from Rishtan went to Riga on a two-month program to learn the ceramic techniques of the Baltic regions. On their return they started working with brown and brown-green colours. However, this style was not popular within the Central Asian region, and after three years these practices ceased due to lack of demand. In 1975, an Usto Association was established by the state, which united all the national master craftsmen of Uzbekistan, including the master potters. Associations of national masters were also established under the Union of Artists of Uzbekistan, whose charter stressed the need to save national traditions and the identity of the national masters. The products created by the masters were subsequently distributed via saloon-shops of the Usto organisation all over the Soviet Union, as well as through the international market. Exhibitions were organised under the sponsorship of the Union of Artists and the Ministry of Culture, as were personal exhibitions of national masters. Various conferences, seminars and symposia of potters were organised at the Tashkent ceramics industrial complex.

As soon as Uzbekistan was declared an independent state in 1991, an organisation of national craftsmen, called Hunarmand,

was established by presidential decree with the aim of sustaining and developing the traditional arts. It encompasses all national crafts, more than forty in number. To further contribute to the development of the national applied arts of Uzbekistan, master craftsmen were released from all taxes under a presidential decree of 31 March 1997. Since the years of independence, the applied arts in Uzbekistan generally have experienced a noticeable rise, as demonstrated, for example, by the creation of some seventy home workshops by individual pottery craftsmen in Rishtan. The production of textiles became free of state control and open to independent free market workshops in Margilan and Namangan—here textile masters are now recreating, along with new designs, the old ones of the 1600s and 1700s. UNESCO is also making efforts to save the traditions, styles and technologies of Uzbekistan. In 1998 it started the Blue of Samarkand project aimed at recovering the traditional technologies of natural glazes for application in the restoration of the architectural tiled monuments of Uzbekistan. This project has been followed by the construction of apprenticeship workshop-schools in the house of the oldest Uzbek master restorer Abdullo Fayziev, in the house-museum of Ahat Muzaffarov in Shakhrisabz in Kashkadarya, in the workshop of Gofirjon Marajapov in Gurumsaray in the Ferghana Valley and in the workshop of the sons of Odilbek Matchanov in Khiva in Khorezm. ☐

TRANSLATED FROM RUSSIAN BY SVETLANA OSIPOVA
AND GUY PETHERBRIDGE, 2004

Opposite: platter detail (see page 137)

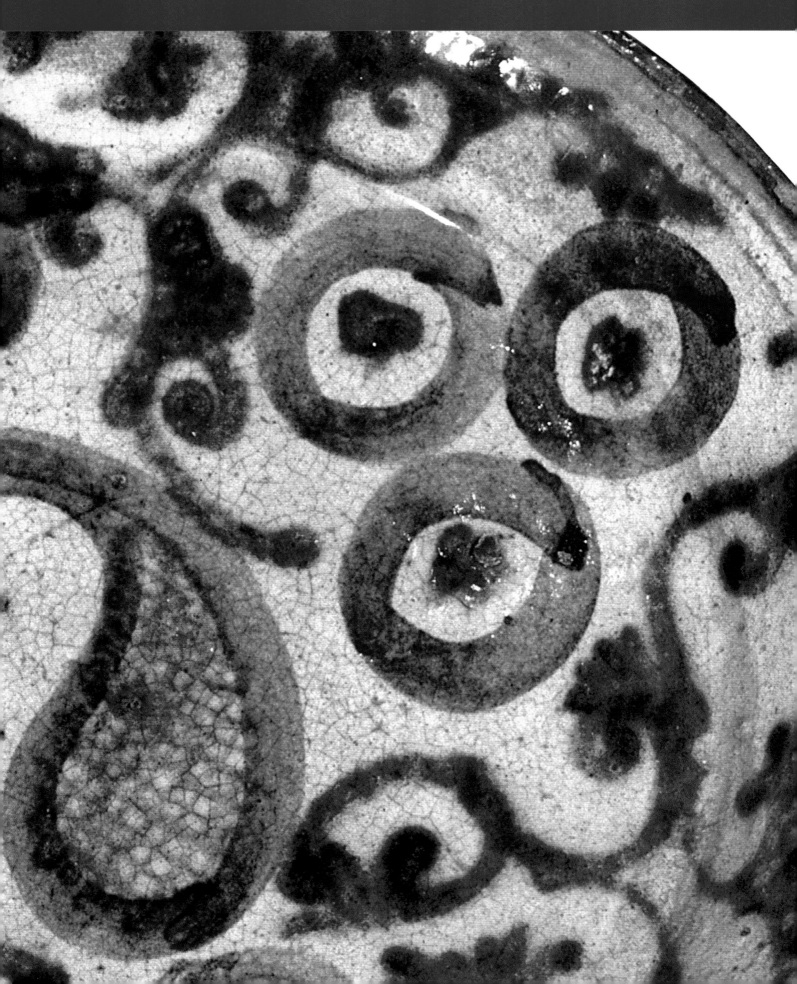

Ewer fragment (left) and **two-handled flask**
Earthenware is a versatile, robust material used over millennia for diverse practical and ritual purposes throughout Central Asia. During the Islamic period light-coloured bodies with a low iron content were generally preferred. Artifacts were often ornamented with mould impressed, incised, combed, carved and applied clay elements.

● Upper body of ewer (left): earthenware, moulded body with looped handle and thumbstop, incised and moulded designs, wood-kiln fired, excavated at Otrar, Southern Kazakhstan, 1200s–1300s. 20 x 18.8 cm

● Flask (right): earthenware, moulded body with attached looped handles, moulded designs, wood-kiln fired, excavated at Termez, Uzbekistan, 1100s. 31.5 x 24 cm

Loop-handled jug (left) and **drink pitcher**
The early Islamic ceramics of southern Tajikistan and northern and central Afghanistan share the pottery making technologies and general formal styles developed in the 10th and 11th centuries in the neighbouring regions of Islamic Central Asia. These vessels are fine examples of utilitarian earthenware from that period.
● Jug (left) and pitcher (right): wheel-thrown earthenware with attached handle, wood-kiln fired, excavated at Khulbok, Khatlon region, Tajikistan, 10th–11th century.

Loop-handled ewer (left) and **jug**

Prior to the introduction of the potter's wheel and the kiln, pots were handbuilt and open fired. These traditions survive in the inaccessible mountainous southern regions and Pamirs of Tajikistan. These vessels are unpainted, the ewer's form reflecting a metal prototype.

● Ewer (left): earthenware, hand-formed, incised and applied clay decorative elements, kiln-fired, globular body, slightly flared neck, angled strut supporting spout, flared footring, made by Masteritza Sabzigul Karimova, Dungara, Khatlon region, Tajikistan, 1980. 27.5 x 17 cm

● Jug (right): earthenware, hand-formed, incised and applied clay decorative elements, kiln-fired, made by Masteritza Sabzigul Karimova, Dungara, Khatlon region, Tajikistan, 1980. 30 x 20.4 cm.

MUSEUM OF ETHNOGRAPHY, DUSHANBE, TAJIKISTAN, 1199-11 (EWER) AND 1199-8 (JUG). PHOTOS BY GENNADY RATUSHENKO

Loop-handled ewers (top) and **pitchers** (below)

Potters in two remote communities of southern Uzbekistan, Kasbi and Kasan, continue to produce earthenware vessels of ancient form. Water is cooled by evaporation through the porous walls—a boon in the fierce summers of the region. The ewers of Kasan, together with small earthenware bowls, are used solely for the ritual washing of the dead.

● Ewer (above left) and pitchers (below left and right): earthenware, wheel-thrown, incised patterns, wood-kiln fired, made by Usto Bakhtiyor Sottorov (1953–), Kasbi, Kashkadarya region, Uzbekistan, 2002. 27 x 18 cm (above left), 21 x 14.5 cm (below left) and 18.5 x 14.5 cm (below right)

● Ewer (above right): earthenware, wheel-thrown, incised patterns, gas-kiln fired, made by Usto Davronov, Kasan, Kashkadarya region, Uzbekistan, 2002. 27 x 17.5 cm

Jugs and bowl

A few female potters in the isolated Pamir mountain valleys of south-eastern Tajikistan continue to hand-build ceramics for family and neighbours. In some areas these are painted with ground earth pigments in geometrical patterns in ancient styles with affinities to regional textile designs.

● Earthenware, hand-formed, red-brown slip-painted, open-fired excavated at Kofarnikhon, Khatlon region, Tajikistan, 11th century. 24.5 x 19 cm

● Jug: earthenware, hand-formed, red-brown slip-painted, open-fired, Sari-seg, Dashtidzum district, Khatlon region, Tajikistan, 1940. 24.5 x 19 cm
● Bowl: earthenware, hand-formed, rounded wall, interior and exterior red slip-painted, open-fired, Sari-seg, Dashtidzum district, Khatlon region, Tajikistan, 1948. 5.5 x 13.8 cm

Animal-form whistles

Many of the surviving pottery workshops in Central Asia continue to produce toy clay whistles (*hushtak*) for the old and popular spring celebration of Navroz. Their forms perpetuate traditionally popular animals.

● Stag form (above): hand-formed earthenware, whistle at side, applied clay decorative elements, wood kiln-fired, painted after firing in red and blue over a white slip, made by Usto Fatkhulla Sadullaev (1886-1956), Uba, Vabkent district, Bukhara region, Uzbekistan, acquired in 1977. 17 x 11.5 cm

MUSEUM OF ETHNOGRAPHY, DUSHANBE, TAJIKISTAN 1126-6 DME45. PHOTO BY GENNADY RATUSHENKO

● Ram (below left) and dog (below right) forms: hand-formed earthenware, whistle at side, kiln-fired, painted after firing in red and blue, made by Usto Djabbar Rakhimov, Uba, Vabkent district, Bukhara region, Uzbekistan, 2004. Approx 12 x 10.5 cm

GUY PETHERBRIDGE COLLECTION: PHOTOS SOTHA BOURN, POWERHOUSE MUSEUM

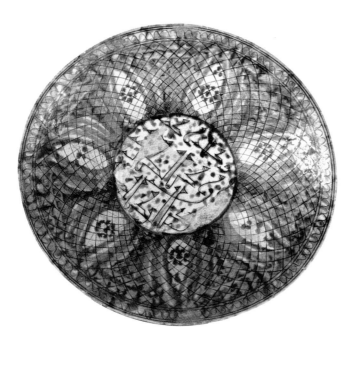

Plates and **bowl**

With the introduction of Islam to Central Asia came new technologies, including a range of coloured glazes for ceramics. The period from the 9th–11th century was one of great creative inventiveness and diversity of ceramic form and design, laying the foundation for a millennium of future potters in the region.

● Plate (above left): alkaline-glazed earthenware, interior underglaze painted in green and light brown-purple on an opaque white silaceous slip ground, neutral-coloured covering glaze, mid 9th century. 5.5 x 34 cm

● Plate (above right): lead-glazed earthenware, interior underglaze painted in green, yellow and light brown-purple on an opaque white siliceous slip ground, neutral-coloured covering glaze, mid 9th century. 5 x 28 cm

● Plate (below left): alkaline-glazed earthenware, interior underglaze painted in blue and black on a white silaceous slip ground, 9th century. 6 x 20 cm

● Bowl (below right): glazed earthenware, interior underglaze painted in brown and black on a white slip ground, 10th century. 5.4 x 17.5 cm

All pieces were excavated at Afrasiab, Samarkand, Uzbekistan; they are wheel-thrown and wood-kiln fired.

Bowl (above) and **plate**

During the 10th and 11th centuries across Central Asia a range of plates and bowls was produced bearing Arabic inscriptions praising Allah, expressing benedictions and exhorting proper behaviour. They are a testament to the spiritual devotion of the period and to the technical skills of the region's potters in producing calligraphy on clay.

● Bowl (above): glazed earthenware, wheel-thrown, interior underglaze painted in red, black and green on a buff slip ground, Arabic inscription at centre 'may the owner be blessed', wood-kiln fired, excavated at Afrasiab, Samarkand, Uzbekistan, late 10th century. 7 x 29 cm

● Plate (left): glazed earthenware with footring, wheel-thrown, interior underglaze painted in red and black on a buff slip ground, Arabic inscription 'blessings', wood-kiln fired, excavated at Afrasiab, Samarkand, Uzbekistan, 10th century. 5 x 37 cm

Jars and **cup**

Central Asian potters of the early Islamic period drew on forms and technologies popular amongst their regional neighbours. The *albarello* was a standard Middle Eastern-style storage jar which has been found throughout Central Asia. The handled cup reflects a metal form current in precious metals in Tang period China and later.

- Jar (*albarello*) (left): glazed earthenware, wheel-thrown, interior underglaze painted in red and brown-black on a white slip ground, floriated Arabic inscription 'ease', slip-incised design contouring, wood-kiln fired, excavated at Afrasiab, Samarkand, Uzbekistan, 10th century. 18.3 x 10 cm

SAMARKAND STATE MUSEUM OF HISTORY AND ARCHITECTURE, UZBEKISTAN, A-2-12. PHOTO BY KONSTANTIN MINAYCHENKO

- Jar (*albarello*) (above right): glazed earthenware, wheel-thrown, with footring, interior underglaze painted in black on a white slip ground, Arabic inscription 'happiness', wood-kiln fired, excavated at Ura Tube, Sogd region, Tajikistan, 10th–12th century. 6 x 14 cm

NATIONAL MUSEUM OF ANTIQUITIES, DUSHANBE, TAJIKISTAN. PHOTO BY GENNADY RATUSHENKO

- Cup (below right): glazed earthenware, wheel-thrown, with footring, interior underglaze painted in black and red on a white slip ground, wood-kiln fired, excavated at Otrar, southern Kazakhstan, 10th–11th century. 7 x 13 cm (including handle)

A.K MARGULAN INSTITUTE OF ARCHAEOLOGY, ACADEMY OF SCIENCES, ALMATY, KAZAKHSTAN, UKKAE KP-T-81 R.III YAMA-33, YAR.1 2476. PHOTO BY OLEG BELYALOV

Plate (above) and **bowl**
Among the most sublime Islamic ceramic creations are the white or buff plates and bowls with Arabic inscriptions in a rich black or brown-black Kufic or Abbasid calligraphy. Long known from Nishapur and Afrasiab, they are also found across Central Asia, both as sophisticated works from major urban centres and rustic products from remoter areas.

● Plate (above): glazed earthenware, wheel-thrown, interior underglaze painted in black on a white slip ground, Arabic inscriptions, wood-kiln fired, exterior glaze over white ground, excavated in southern Kazakhstan, 11th–12th century. 4.5 x 28 cm

A.K MARGULAN INSTITUTE OF ARCHAEOLOGY, ACADEMY OF SCIENCES, ALMATY, KAZAKHSTAN, K-R-T-82 YAMA-13 YAR-7 2101 331. PHOTO BY OLEG BELYALOV

● Bowl (below): earthenware, wheel-thrown, interior painted in black on a buff slip ground, Arabic inscriptions, wood-kiln fired, exterior buff slip painted, excavated at Khulbok, Khatlon region, Tajikistan, 10th–11th century.

NATIONAL MUSEUM OF ANTIQUITIES, DUSHANBE, TAJIKISTAN. PHOTO BY GUY PETHERBRIDGE

Plates
The painted underglaze decoration of this design genre—featuring massive, opposed palmettes, opposed Arabic inscriptions and minor decorative elements—was very popular across Central Asia from the 10th to 11th century.
● (Above) Glazed earthenware, wheel-thrown, interior underglaze painted in brown, black and grey on a white slip ground, Arabic inscription, wood-kiln fired, excavated at Taraz, southern Kazakhstan, 11th–12th century. 7.8 x 36 cm

● (Below) Glazed earthenware, wheel-thrown, interior underglaze painted in red and black on a white slip ground, pseudo-Arabic inscription, slip-incised patterns, wood-kiln fired, excavated at Afrasiab, Samarkand, Uzbekistan, 9th century. 6 x 19 cm

Bowls (above and opposite)
The great first period of Central Asian glazed ceramic inventiveness of the 9th to 11th centuries saw the refinement of painting in mineral slips under a transparent glaze—often incorporating benedictory Arabic inscriptions or pseudo-inscriptions or depictions of birds or animals of a propitious nature.
● Restored, straight, flaring wall, flat base, glazed earthenware, wheel-thrown, interior underglaze painted in red and white on a dark blue-black slip ground, Arabic inscription 'happiness', exterior unglazed, wood-kiln fired, excavated at Afrasiab, Samarkand, Uzbekistan, early 11th century. 8 x 26 cm

● (Above): glazed earthenware, wheel-thrown, interior underglaze painted in brown red, light olive-green and white on a red-brown slip ground, exterior similarly treated, Arabic inscription 'happiness', wood kiln-fired, excavated at Afrasiab, Samarkand, Uzbekistan, late 10th–early 11th century. 7.5 x 24 cm

● (Below left): glazed earthenware, wheel-thrown, interior underglaze painted in black, white and olive-green on a red-brown slip ground, exterior similarly treated, wood kiln-fired, excavated at Afrasiab, Samarkand, Uzbekistan, late 10th–early 11th century. 8.5 x 27 cm

● (Below right): glazed earthenware, wheel-thrown, interior underglaze painted in black, white and olive-green on a red-brown ground, wood kiln-fired, excavated at Afrasiab, Samarkand, Uzbekistan, late 10th–early 11th century. 8 x 23 cm

SAMARKAND STATE MUSEUM OF HISTORY AND ARCHITECTURE, UZBEKISTAN, A-398-1, A-49-155, A-49-142. PHOTOS BY KONSTANTIN MINAYCHENKO

Aquamaniles (water pourers)

Metal aquamaniles of zoomorphic form were popular in medieval Islamic culture. In Central Asia from the 10th century to the present day they were also created in glazed earthenware. In recent centuries the most popular have been in the form of ducks, roosters and camels.

● (Right) Glazed earthenware, hand-formed, three-footed, loop-handled water vessel in form of a bird and the head of a monkey or a person as a spout, underglaze painted in brown-red, black and green on a light slip ground, scored and carved decorative roundels, wood-kiln fired, excavated at Kalan Kakhkakha, Khatlon region, Tajikistan, 10th century. 24.5 x 15 x 24 cm

NATIONAL MUSEUM OF ANTIQUITIES, DUSHANBE, TAJIKISTAN 204/2454. PHOTO BY GENNADY RATUSHENKO

● (Left) Long, ovoid body, looped handle, prominent footring, glazed earthenware, body wheel-thrown, other elements hand-built, underglaze painted in green and yellow over a white slip ground, wood-kiln fired, made in Andijon (Abduvakhobov workshop), Uzbekistan, early 1900s. 22 x 30.5 cm

MIRZABAKHROM ABDUVAKHOBOV COLLECTION. PHOTO BY GUY PETHERBRIDGE

Dishes

A feature of Central Asian glazed ceramics in the 9th to 10th centuries was the slip or chemical underglaze painting of vessels with abstract or geometrical patterns reflecting textile designs—differing quite markedly from the genres using calligraphy, anthropomorphic or zoomorphic motifs.

• (Above) Rounded wall, glazed earthenware, wheel-thrown, interior underglaze painted in dark-brown and black on a white slip ground, slip-incised patterns, wood-kiln fired, excavated at Afrasiab, Samarkand, Uzbekistan, late 10th century. 7 x 26.7 cm

• (Left) Rounded wall, glazed earthenware, wheel-thrown, interior underglaze painted in red-brown, black and green a light slip ground, wood-kiln fired, excavated at Afrasiab, Samarkand, Uzbekistan, late 9th–early 10th century. 6 x 20 cm

Jug (above) and **dish**

By the 10th century potters across Central Asia were masking earthenware bodies with a fine light-coloured slip as a ground for painting with chemical glazes or mineral slips under a neutral-coloured transparent covering glaze. These were kiln-fired in an oxidising atmosphere. Illustrated is a simple graphic style with pseudo calligraphic inscriptions on a light ground.

● Jug (above): flaring footring, glazed earthenware, wheel-thrown, exterior underglaze painted in black and red on a white slip ground, interior white underglaze, wood-kiln fired, excavated at Afrasiab, Samarkand, Uzbekistan, first half of the 10th century. 15.5 x 14 cm

SAMARKAND STATE MUSEUM OF HISTORY AND ARCHITECTURE, UZBEKISTAN, A-49-582. PHOTO BY KONSTANTIN MINAYCHENKO

● Dish (below): glazed earthenware, wheel-thrown, interior underglaze painted in brown-black on a white slip ground, wood-kiln fired, excavated in Southern Kazakhstan, 11th–12th century. 4.5 x 17 cm

A.K MARGULAN INSTITUTE OF ARCHAEOLOGY, ACADEMY OF SCIENCES, ALMATY, KAZAKHSTAN, 0-84 III. PHOTO BY OLEG BELYALOV

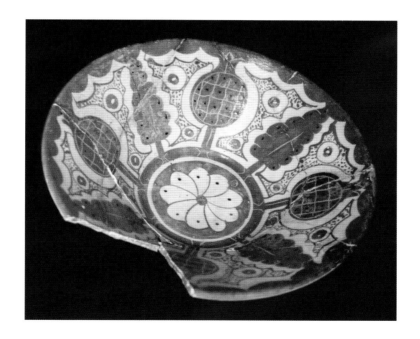

Bowls

While much of the ceramic technology characteristic of early Islamic Central Asia became a common regional vocabulary, some achievements were never repeated, such as these pure olive green and vermilion red glazes on a lustrous white ground, found across Central Asia in the 10th to 11th centuries.

● (Above) Flaring wall, flat base, glazed earthenware, wheel-thrown, interior underglaze painted in olive green and red on a white slip ground, exterior same white slip ground under glaze, wood-kiln fired, excavated at Kuiruktobe, Kazakhstan, 11th century. 11x 24 cm

A.K. MARGULAN INSTITUTE OF ARCHAEOLOGY, ACADEMY OF SCIENCES, ALMATY, KAZAKHSTAN. PHOTO BY OLEG BELYALOV

● (Below) Glazed earthenware, wheel-thrown, interior underglaze painted in olive green and red on a white slip ground, wood-kiln fired, excavated at Khulbok district, Khatlon region, Tajikistan, 10th–11th century. 10.5 x 28.5 cm

NATIONAL MUSEUM OF ANTIQUITIES, DUSHANBE, TAJIKISTAN, KP 1189/73. PHOTO BY GENNADY RATUSHENKO

Bowl

Between the 11th and 14th centuries lustre wares were produced in a number of Iranian centres. Current evidence indicates that lustre glazes were not produced in Central Asia. This vessel was an import from Rayy, Kashan or another provincial Iranian kiln.

● Glazed ware, wheel-thrown, narrow footring, double fired—first firing of a transparent glaze over a white ground—then lustre painted and fired again at a lower temperature, wood-kiln fired, excavated at Kalan Bolo, Isfara district, Sogd region, Tajikistan, late 1100s–early 1200s. 15 x 25 cm

Bottles

Tall, elegant bottles and vases in monochrome glazes over a stonepaste or earthenware body were a popular feature of late and post medieval Iranian Islamic culture and neighbouring Central Asia. They are frequently depicted in scenes of courtly and heroic life in Timurid and Shaibanid manuscript painting.

● (Left and right) Footring, alkaline-glazed stonepaste, wheel-thrown, monochrome blue glaze, kiln-fired, Karakalpakstan, Uzbekistan, 1200s–1300s. 28 x 10 cm

Storage jar

A genre of ceramics produced by potters in centres across Central Asia exploited the effects created by a lead glaze over a light toned slip ground painted in various red and brown mineral glazes and slips. Antimony oxide sometimes enhanced the yellow tone.

● Footring, glazed earthenware, wheel-thrown, exterior underglaze painted in a dark brown and a lighter brown on a light-toned slip ground, yellow transparent covering glaze, wood-kiln fired, unknown provenance, Uzbekistan, 1100s. 27 x 18 cm

Bowls

The Mongol dominance over East and Middle Asia and much of the Middle East in the 1200s and 1300s led to further ceramic design developments in Central Asia, drawing on technologies and styles well established there and on designs popular in neighbouring regions.

● (Above left) Lead-glazed earthenware, wheel-thrown, interior underglaze painted in red-brown, green and black on light toned slip ground, yellow transparent covering glaze, exterior painted in black over slip (unglazed), wood-kiln fired, excavated at Otrar, southern Kazakhstan, late 1300s–1400s. 8 x 17 cm

● (Above right) Lead-glazed earthenware, wheel-thrown, interior underglaze painted in red-brown, green and black on light toned slip ground, yellow transparent covering glaze, exterior painted in black over slip (partly glazed), wood-kiln fired, excavated at Otrar, southern Kazakhstan, late 1300s–1400s. 8.2 x 17.5 cm

● (Below left) Alkaline-glazed earthenware, wheel-thrown, interior underglaze painted in black, purple and blue on a white siliceous slip ground, exterior underglaze painted in blue and purple on the same ground, wood-kiln fired, excavated at Otrar, southern Kazakhstan, late 1300s–1400s. 8 x 19.5 cm

● (Below right) Alkaline-glazed earthenware, wheel-thrown, interior underglaze painted in purple-black and blue on a white siliceous slip ground, exterior underglaze painted in blue and purple on same white ground, wood-kiln fired, excavated at Otrar, southern Kazakhstan, late 1300s–1400s. 8 x 17.5 cm

Bowls

Following the Mongol invasions, Central Asia began new trade and other relationships with its neighbours. The design of the bowl (above) drew on Chinese prototypes and was popular in various centres including Saraichik in Kazakhstan, while the bowl (below) illustrates an Iranian influence.

● (Above left and right) Small, slightly everted footring, alkaline-glazed earthenware, wheel-thrown, interior and exterior underglaze painted in black, blue and light purple-brown on white siliceous slip ground, wood-kiln fired, excavated at Samarkand, Uzbekistan, 1300s. 8.5 x 18 cm

● (Below) Footring, alkaline-glazed earthenware, wheel-thrown, interior and exterior underglaze painted in blue and black on a white siliceous slip ground, wood-kiln fired, excavated at Saraichik, Kazakhstan, 1200s–1300s. 5.5 x 18 cm

Plate (above) and **plate fragments**

During the late Timurid and Shaibanid periods of the 1400s and 1500s, Chinese motifs transmitted through Chinese textiles and ceramics and Islamic copies were transformed into a distinctly indigenous design vocabulary.

● (Above) Glazed stonepaste ware, wheel-thrown, interior underglaze painted in blues on a white siliceous slip ground, wood-kiln fired, excavated at Tashkent, Uzbekistan, 1400s. 4 x 27 cm

STATE MUSEUM OF TEMURID HISTORY, TASHKENT, UZBEKISTAN, 2-75

● (Below left) Glazed earthenware, wheel-thrown, interior underglaze painted in blue and black on a white ground, wood-kiln fired, excavated at Samarkand, Uzbekistan, 1300s.

STATE MUSEUM OF TEMURID HISTORY, TASHKENT, UZBEKISTAN, KP 2-74 A 1-35

● (Below right) Alkaline-glazed earthenware, wheel-thrown, interior underglaze painted in blue and purple-black on a white siliceous slip ground, wood-kiln fired, excavated at Samarkand, Uzbekistan, 1400s.

SAMARKAND STATE MUSEUM OF HISTORY AND ARCHITECTURE, UZBEKISTAN, A-608-2. PHOTOS BY KONSTANTIN MINAYCHENKO

Plate (above) and **bowl** (opposite)
During the rule of Amir Timur (1336–1405) and his successors there was renewed interest in the decorative arts of China. Blue and white porcelain wares were developed in China for a largely Middle Eastern Muslim market, influencing new trends in Islamic ceramics and those of Central Asia.
● Glazed stonepaste, wheel-thrown, interior underglaze painted in blues on a white siliceous slip ground, wood-kiln fired, excavated at Ulugbek Madrasa, Samarkand, Uzbekistan, 1400s. 7 x 40 cm

● Restored, footring, alkaline-glazed stonepaste, wheel-thrown, interior and exterior underglaze painted in blue and black on a white siliceous slip ground, wood-kiln fired, excavated at Samarkand, Uzbekistan, 1400s. 9.2 x 19 cm

Plate (above), **dish** and **bowl** (following pages)
The shift in the political environment in Central Asia (from the mid 1500s to the mid 1800s) from successive phases of dominance over neighbouring Islamic regions to a more relatively internal looking culture is reflected in the ceramics in the development of distinctly local styles.
● Alkaline-glazed earthenware, wheel-thrown, underglaze painted in blue and black on a white siliceous slip ground, wood-kiln fired, excavated at Samarkand, Uzbekistan, 1500s. 6 x 24 cm

● Dish: alkaline-glazed earthenware, wheel-thrown, underglaze painted in blue and black on a white siliceous ground, wood-kiln fired, Rishtan, Ferghana region, Uzbekistan, 1800s. 6 x 30 cm

● Bowl: footring, alkaline-glazed earthenware, wheel-thrown, underglaze painted in blue and purple on a white siliceous slip ground, wood-kiln fired, excavated at Samarkand, Uzbekistan, 1500s. 5 x 28 cm

STATE MUSEUM OF TEMURID HISTORY, TASHKENT, UZBEKISTAN, 74/4. PHOTO BY KONSTANTIN MINAYCHENKO

Bowls

During the 1830s and 1890s the Chinese consolidated control over Kashgar and the Tarim Basin and promoted links with Muslims to the west. Admired Qing dynasty porcelains were copied and transformed into the distinctive *chinni* ware of the Ferghana Valley, Uzbekistan.

● (Above left) Footring, alkaline-glazed earthenware, wheel-thrown, underglaze painted in blue on an opaque white siliceous slip ground, wood-kiln fired, acquired in Khudjand, Tajikistan, 1800s. 8.6 x 17.5 cm

● (Above right) Alkaline-glazed earthenware, wheel-thrown, underglaze painted in blue and purple on a white siliceous slip ground, wood-kiln fired, Isfara district, Sogd region, Tajikistan, late 1800s. 10.5 x 19 cm

● (Below) Prominent conical pedestal footring, glazed earthenware, wheel-thrown, underglaze painted in blue and black on a white siliceous slip ground, wood-kiln fired, made in Chorku, Isfara district, Sogd region, Tajikistan, late 1800s. 13.2 x 21 cm

MUSEUM OF ETHNOGRAPHY, DUSHANBE, TAJIKISTAN, 1314-81 (ABOVE LEFT), 641-161 (ABOVE RIGHT) AND 641-50 (BELOW). PHOTOS BY GENNADY RATUSHENKO

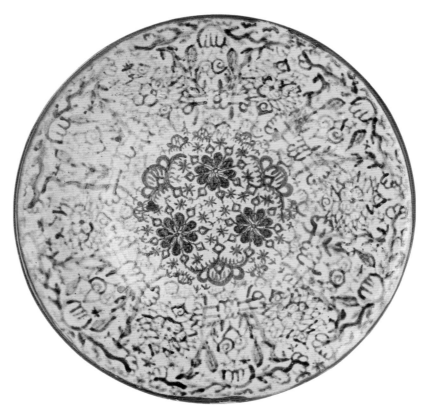

Platters

Central Asian potters had a ready market for plates for *plov*, the communally shared rice dish. Tajik potters produced large platters for *plov* in *chinni* ware, drawing on 1800s Qing designs, a style continued by the few surviving potters of northern Tajikistan.

● (Above left) Alkaline-glazed earthenware, wheel-thrown, underglaze painted in blue and purple on a white siliceous ground, wood-kiln fired, Kanibadam, Sogd region , Tajikistan, latter 1800s. 4.6 x 32.5 cm

● (Above right) Alkaline-glazed earthenware, wheel-thrown, underglaze painted in blue and purple on a white siliceous slip ground, wood-kiln fired, made in Khudjand, Tajikistan, late 1800s. 4.5 x 34 cm

● (Below) Alkaline-glazed earthenware, wheel-thrown, underglaze painted in blue and purple on a white siliceous slip ground, gas-kiln fired, made by Usto Safarboi Sokibov (1925–), Chorku, Isfara district, Sogd region, Tajikistan, 1980s. 3.7 x 38.8 cm

Bowls

The only potter in Tajikistan now producing glazed ware in a fully traditional context is Usto Safarboi Sokibov. Now in his late 70s, he lives in the village of Chorku in the Isfara district of northern Tajikistan (once a flourishing ceramic centre) where he still produces bowls and platters in the *chinni* style—the last true survivor of the ceramic Silk Road.

● (Above right) Bulbous footring, glazed earthenware, wheel-thrown, underglaze painted in blue on a white slip ground, gas-kiln fired, made by Usto Safarboi Sokibov (1925–), Chorku, Isfara district, Sogd region, Tajikistan, 1970s. 8.2 x 16.5 cm

● (Centre) Bulbous footring, glazed earthenware, wheel-thrown, underglaze painted in blue and purple-brown on a white ground, gas-kiln fired, made by Usto Safarboi Sokibov, Chorku, Isfara district, Sogd region, Tajikistan, 1990s. 8 x 16 cm

● (Below right) Bulbous footring, glazed earthenware, wheel-thrown, underglaze painted in blue on a white ground, gas-kiln fired, made by Usto Safarboi Sokibov, Chorku, Isfara district, Sogd region, Tajikistan, 1990s. 8.8 x 16.5 cm

GUY PETHERBRIDGE COLLECTION. PHOTOS BY SOTHA BOURN, POWERHOUSE MUSEUM

Platters and **plate** (above)

Just as the offering and sharing of *plov* is a basic social custom across Central Asia, so the offering of tea to guests is a necessary duty of hospitality. Both customs are reflected in these large *chinni*-style *plov* platters from northern Tajikistan. The knife depicted is an apotropaic (protective) symbol.

● (Opposite top and bottom left) Alkaline-glazed earthenware, wheel-thrown, underglaze painted on a white siliceous slip ground, exterior white underglaze painted on the same ground, wood-kiln fired, made at Chorku, Isfara district, Sogd region, Tajikistan, early 1900s. 8.9 x 51 cm (top) and 8 x 50 cm (bottom left)

● (Opposite bottom right) Alkaline-glazed earthenware, footring, wheel-thrown, interior underglaze painted in blues on a white siliceous slip ground, exterior underglaze painted on same ground, wood-kiln fired, made by Usto Goib, Chorku, Isfara district, Sogd region, Tajikistan, late 1800s. 6 x 44.5 cm

● (Above) Alkaline-glazed earthenware, wheel-thrown, Chorku, Isfara district, Sogd region, Tajikistan, 1957. 5.8 x 27.5 cm

MUSEUM OF ETHNOGRAPHY, DUSHANBE, TAJIKISTAN 664-136 (ABOVE), 641-26 (CENTRE) AND 917-165 (BELOW). PHOTOS BY GENNADY RATUSHENKO

Plates, platter and bowl

These blue-green vessels are produced by copper oxide on a white siliceous slip ground under an alkaline glaze fluxed with *ishkor*, a local plant ash. They are among the last works of Gurumsaray master, Usto Maksudali Turopov (1932–1998), while Usto Mahmud Rakhimov has not worked for two decades. These pieces demonstrate the characteristic freedom to vary decoration.

● Plate (above left): footring, alkaline-glazed earthenware, wheel-thrown, interior and exterior underglaze painted in blue-green on a white siliceous slip ground, kiln-fired, made by Usto Mahmud Rakhimov. 6 x 28.6 cm

● Platter (above right), plate (below left) and bowl (below right): footring, alkaline-glazed earthenware, wheel-thrown, underglaze painted in blue-green on a white siliceous slip ground, kiln-fired, made by Usto Maksudali Turopov. 7.5 x 40 cm (above right), 4 x 28.2 cm (below left) and 9.6 x 27.3 cm (below right). All are from Gurumsaray, Papsky district, Namangan region, Uzbekistan, 1980s.

Plate

This plate of the Andijon master, Usto Mirzabakhrom Abduvakhobov, is alkaline-glazed over a white clay and siliceous slip ground. Copper oxide produces the blue-green and manganese dioxide the purple. The design is based on the waterwheel and burgeoning vegetation, symbolising abundance and annual cycles of regeneration.

⬤ Alkaline-glazed earthenware, wheel-thrown, underglaze painted in blue and purple on a white siliceous slip ground, gas-kiln fired, made by Usto Mirzabakhrom Abduvakhobov (1950–), Andijon, Uzbekistan, 1993. 4.3 x 32.8 cm

Platter

This platter from northern Tajikistan illustrates the technical mastery of Kanibadam potters of the late 1800s in controlling alkaline glazes and in firing large items. The design in white reserve against a brilliant green-blue demonstrates how creatively local potters could reinterpret Chinese prototypes.
● Alkaline-glazed earthenware, wheel-thrown, underglaze painted in green-blue and purple on a white siliceous slip ground, exterior glazed over the same ground, wood-kiln fired, made by Usto Meli, Chorku, Isfara district, Sogd region, Tajikistan, late 1800s. 5.8 x 51 cm

Platters

Throughout the history of Central Asian glazed ceramics there has been interplay between ceramic decoration and textile designs. These *plov* platters from the Ferghana Valley (now divided between Tajikistan and Uzbekistan) use motifs such as *bodums*, chillis, flowers and serrated leafy scrolls commonly associated with textiles, particularly embroideries and textile block prints.

● (Above) Alkaline-glazed earthenware, wheel-thrown, underglaze painting in blue and purple on a white siliceous slip ground, wood-kiln fired, made in Kokand, Ferghana region, Uzbekistan, 1930. 5 x 4 cm

SAMARKAND STATE MUSEUM OF HISTORY AND ARCHITECTURE, UZBEKISTAN, KP 3839/15. PHOTO BY KONSTANTIN MINAYCHENKO

● (Below left and right) Alkaline-glazed earthenware, wheel-thrown, underglaze painting in blue and purple-black on a white siliceous slip ground, wood-kiln fired, made at Chorku, Isfara district, Sogd region, Tajikistan, early 1900s. Platter on right made by Usto Abdunabi or Usto Adugani 7.3 x 43 cm (left) and 5.2 x 31 cm (right)

MUSEUM OF ETHNOGRAPHY, DUSHANBE, TAJIKISTAN, 664-199 (LEFT) AND 664-114 (RIGHT). PHOTOS BY GENNADY RATUSHENKO

Hand washing basins

In Islamic Central Asia the washing of hands symbolises purification and hospitality towards guests. Water is poured from a metal or ceramic ewer and collected in a metal or ceramic basin. These may be elaborately decorated or very simple, as in the case of this small basin from Boysun. The Shakhrisabz basin shares the colours of the local head shawl (*paranja*) embroideries.

● (Above) Glazed earthenware, wheel-thrown, glazed on body without slip, wood-kiln fired, made by Usto Eshonkulov Izzatullo, Boysun, Sukhandarya region, Uzbekistan, 1970s. 11 x 18 cm

GUY PETHERBRIDGE COLLECTION. PHOTO BY GUY PETHERBRIDGE

● (Below) Lead-glazed earthenware, wheel-thrown, underglaze slip painting in browns, reds and yellows on a white slip ground, wood-kiln fired, made in Shakhrisabz or Kitab, Kashkadarya region, Uzbekistan, 1950s

I.V SAVITSKY STATE MUSEUM OF ART OF THE REPUBLIC OF KARAKALPAKSTAN, NUKUS, 130 X 130 CM. PHOTO BY KONSTANTIN MINAYCHENKO

Bottle, puzzle ewer and **two-handled jar**

Potters in Samarkand, Shakhrisabz and Kitab use freely-drawn underglaze painting made lustrous by the amber-toned covering lead glazes to create designs sharing motifs with local embroideries of these areas, including the characteristic split palmettes, floriated scrolls and serrated leaf forms.

● Bottle (left): lead-glazed earthenware, wheel-thrown, underglaze slip painting in red-brown, blue and green on a light toned slip ground, made by Usto Murodov, Samarkand, Uzbekistan, 1930s. 27 x 15 cm

● Puzzle ewer (spout broken off) (above right): filled with water from a hole in base, lead-glazed earthenware, moulded and luted components, underglaze slip painting in browns, reds, yellows and greens on a white slip ground, made by Usto Azim Hotamov, Shakhrisabz, Kashkadarya region, Uzbekistan, 1970s. 33.5 x 17.2 cm

● Two-handled jar (below right): lead-glazed earthenware, wheel-thrown, wood-kiln fired, Kitab, Kashkadarya region, Uzbekistan, 1951. 35 x 23 cm

Platter (above) and **hand-washing basin**

The pottery traditions of Urgut in Samarkand province and Denau in adjacent Sukhandarya use lead glazes and copper and iron underglaze splashes with slip-incised patterns, which are found amongst early glazed ceramic productions in Iraq of the 8th to 10th centuries.

● (Above) Platter: lead-glazed earthenware, wheel-thrown, interior green and brown on a white slip ground, slip-incised patterns, exterior underglaze painted in green on the same ground, amber lead covering glaze, wood-kiln fired, made by Usto Mukhammad Rasul Zukhurov (1930–), Denau, Sukhandarya region, Uzbekistan, 2004. 5.2 x 33.5 cm

● (Below) Hand-washing basin: lead-glazed earthenware, wheel-thrown, interior underglaze painted green and brown on a white slip ground, slip-incised patterns, amber lead glaze, exterior underglaze painted in open turquoise green over a white slip ground, wood-kiln fired (fired upside down), made by Usto Mukhammad Rasul Zukhurov (1930–), Denau, Sukhandarya region, Uzbekistan, 1960s. 11 x 30.5 cm

Platter

The Ablakulov pottery workshop of Urgut, a hill town famous for its embroideries, continues an ancient Islamic tradition of lead-glazed ceramics such as bottles, bowls, plates and platters. This platter uses an underglaze decorated with copper oxide with green trails from the rim into the well.

● Lead-glazed earthenware, wheel-thrown, interior underglaze decorated by green slip trails, exterior wall green glazed, slip-incised patterns, amber lead covering glaze, wood-kiln fired (fired upside down), made by Usto No'mon Ablakulov (1964–), Urgut, Samarkand region province, Uzbekistan, 2001.

5.3 x 48.2 cm

Platters (above and opposite)

Gizduvan has remained an important centre of ceramic production in. Although no longer producing ceramics, Kattakurgan supported a flourishing industry until the 1970s, sharing many designs and practices with Gizduvan and Samarkand. The multi-coloured lead-glazed wares designs draw on local textile traditions.

● Lead-glazed earthenware, wheel-thrown, underglaze painted in blue, brown, yellow, white and green on a black ground, made by Usto I Narzullaev, Gizduvan, Bukhara region, Uzbekistan, 1974. 5 x 36 cm

Glazed earthenware, wheel-thrown, underglaze painted in blue, buff, yellow-ochre, red and green on a black ground, wood-kiln fired (fired upside down), Kattakurgan, Samarkand region, Uzbekistan, 1920s. 5 x 35 cm

Dishes

Unique in world ceramics are the copper oxide blue on white alkaline glazed vessels of Khorezm province and Karakalpakstan, drawing on medieval Islamic ceramic designs. Khiva and the adjacent Kattabag and Madyr (Khanki) villages were the principal pottery centres serving this populous region.

● (Above left and right, below right) Solid footring, alkaline-glazed earthenware, wheel-thrown, underglaze painted in blue on a white siliceous slip ground, wood-kiln fired, made in Kattabag, Yangiaryk district, Khorezm region, Uzbekistan, 1950s–1960s. 9.8 x 31.5 cm (above left), 9.5 x 32 cm (above right) and 8 x 26.1 cm (below right)

● (Below left) Alkaline-glazed earthenware, wheel-thrown, underglaze painted in blues on a white siliceous slip ground, kiln-fired, Khorezm or Karakalpakstan, Uzbekistan, 1800s. 6.8 x 29 cm

GUY PETHERBRIDGE COLLECTION. PHOTOS BY SOTHA BOURN, POWERHOUSE MUSEUM (ABOVE) AND GUY PETHERBRIDGE (BELOW)

Dish

Most Khorezm painted ceramic designs feature dark elements on a light background (blue on white). Some potters, such as Usto Matyakubov, also create designs in reverse (white on blue) as illustrated here.

● Solid footring, alkaline-glazed earthenware, wheel-thrown, underglaze painted in blue on a white siliceous slip ground, wood-kiln fired, 1950s, made by Usto Matyakubov, Khiva, Khorezm region, Uzbekistan. 10 x 31.5 cm

Dishes

In the 1950s and 1960s, as the population of Khorezm province grew with Soviet irrigation schemes, Khivan potters and others in the area responded with a rich range of colourful designs serving a growing market for *badias*, or dishes for *plov*, sets of which were used for weddings and other celebrations.

● (Above left) Solid footring, interior underglaze painted in black on a white slip ground under a yellow glaze, 1960s. 9 x 29 cm

● (Above right) Solid footring, interior underglaze painted in green, light brown, brown and white and on a white ground, slip-incised patterns, 1970s. 7.9 x 31.8 cm

● (Below left) Solid footring, wheel-thrown, interior underglaze painted in purple-black and green on a white slip ground under a yellow glaze, (fired upside down), 1960s. 8.8 x 30.5 cm

● (Below right) Prominent, solid footring, interior underglaze painted in green, white and red-brown on a white slip ground, slip-incised patterns, 1940s–1950s. 8.5 x 30.5 cm

All were made in the Khiva area, Khorezm region, Uzbekistan; lead-glazed earthenware, wheel-thrown, wood-kiln fired.

GUY PETHERBRIDGE COLLECTION. PHOTOS BY SOTHA BOURN, POWERHOUSE MUSEUM

Dishes

Three of these *plov* dishes or *badias* were produced by Usto Rajab Ortiqov using his 'apple' design in the 1960s. The last (below right) was produced as a recent revival in his workshop and shows the effect of modern equipment such as the glaze ball mill and gas kiln.

● (Above left, above right and below left) Prominent solid footring, lead-glazed earthenware, wheel-thrown, underglaze painting in brown, green and white on a white slip ground under a yellow glaze, slip-incised patterns, wood-kiln fired, made by Usto Rajab Ortiqov, Khiva, Khorezm region, Uzbekistan, 1960s. 9 x 29.6 cm (above left), 9 x 30.5 cm (above right) and 8.3 x 30.5 cm (below left)

● (Below right) Prominent, solid footring lead-glazed earthenware, wheel-thrown, underglaze painting in brown, green and white on a white slip ground under a yellow glaze, slip-incised patterns, gas-kiln fired, made by Usto Rajab Ortiqov, Khiva, Khorezm region, Uzbekistan, 2003. 8.5 x 28.5 cm

Dish

Potters of westernmost Central Asia—in Khorezm province, Kunya Urgench and Karakalpakstan—use designs in blue on white alkaline-glazed wares which have strong, seemingly pre-Islamic elements, bearing a relationship to local jewellery and embroidery traditions.

● Alkaline-glazed earthenware, solid footring, wheel-thrown, underglaze painted in blue on a white siliceous slip ground, wood kiln-fired, made by Usto Eshmurod Sapaev (1925–1996), Kunya Urgench, Turkmenistan, 1970s. 10 x 33 cm

Plate

In the latter decades of the Soviet era, potters and other craftspeople in the Central Asian republics combined new motifs of the modern socialist world with traditional designs. This large plate for *plov* (*badia*) includes the Russian acronym for the Union of Soviet Socialist Republics (CCCP) together with images of a bus, a biplane and other aircraft.

● Alkaline glazed earthenware, wheel-thrown, underglaze painted in blue-green on a white siliceous slip ground, kiln-fired, made by Usto S Kalandarov, Khodjeili, Karakalpakstan, 1960s. 10 x 33 cm

Cooking pots

While Central Asian potters shared many functional ceramic forms with potters elsewhere, they also created vessels of very local character. These upright vessels were made in quite different parts of Uzbekistan where they are used to cook food in the traditional *tandir*.

● Two-handled lidded pot (left): looped handles, collared lid, footring, glazed earthenware, wheel-thrown, exterior underglaze painted in blue on a white slip ground, interior glazed in blue on white ground, gas-kiln fired, made by Usto Ismail Komilov, Rishtan, Ferghana region, Uzbekistan, 1997. 16.2 x 12.5 cm

● Lidded pot (right): footring, lead-glazed earthenware, wheel-thrown, exterior underglaze painted in green and blue on a white slip ground under a transparent yellow glaze, interior yellow glaze over a white ground, gas-kiln fired, made by Usto Abdullo Narzullaev, Gizduvan, Bukhara region, Uzbekistan, 1997. 16.2 x 12 cm

Cradle pots

The *beshik tuvak* is a little glazed earthenware peepot with a broad circular lip used under a baby's cradle. Each traditional working potter in Central Asia still has a good business making *beshik tuvaks*, often hundreds or more a year being produced in each workshop.

● (Above left) Footring, glazed earthenware, wheel-thrown, underglaze painted in black and red-brown on biff slip, wood-kiln-fired, excavated at Taraz, Kazakhstan, 10th–11th century. 15.5 x 9 cm

● (Above centre) Lead-glazed earthenware, wheel-thrown, interior underglaze painted in blue, red and green on a white slip ground, yellow-toned transparent covering glaze, exterior similarly treated but also with carved decoration near base, gas-kiln fired, made by Usto Mirzabakhrom Abduvakhobov (1950–), Andijon, Uzbekistan, 2001. 15 x 9.2 cm

● (Above right) Lead-glazed earthenware, wheel-thrown, interior monochrome green glaze directly onto body (no slip), gas-kiln fired, made by Usto Mukhammad Rasul Zukhurov, Denau, Sukhandarya region, Uzbekistan, 2004. 15.3 x 8.9 cm

● (Below left) Lead-glazed earthenware, wheel-thrown, interior and upper exterior underglaze painted in green and white directly onto body (no slip ground), gas kiln-fired, made by Usto Nazrullo Abdullaev, Kitab, Kashkadarya region, Uzbekistan, 2004. 15.3 cm x 9 cm

● (Below centre) Lead-glazed earthenware, wheel-thrown, interior underglaze painted in white directly onto body (no slip ground), gas-kiln fired, made by Usto Mirzabakhrom Abduvakhobov, (1950–), Andijon, Uzbekistan, 2000. 15 x 8.9 cm

● (Below right) Glazed earthenware, wheel-thrown, interior underglaze painted in blue and purple on a white slip ground, kiln-fired, Tajikistan, 2002. 15.3 cm x 9.2 cm

Storage jars

The two- or four-handled storage jar or *khum* has long been the essential storage container in Central Asia. The vertical design permits efficient use of storage space. In the case of the slender, neck-waisted form without exterior glaze, the design allows for transport by camel, horse and donkey.

● (Left) Lead-glazed earthenware, built from wheel-thrown components, exterior underglaze painted in white and green (no slip background), interior lead glazed (no slip ground), gas-kiln fired, made by Usto Rajab Ortiqov, Khiva, Khorezm region, Uzbekistan, 2002. 47.5 x 17.9 cm

● (Right) Lead-glazed earthenware, built from wheel-thrown components, exterior and interior monochrome green glazed, gas-kiln fired, made by Usto Rajab Ortiqov, Khiva, Khorezm region, Uzbekistan, 2002. 65 x 35.6 cm

Bibliography

General

Adle, C & Habib, I (eds). *History of civilizations of Central Asia, Vol 5: Development in contrast: from the sixteenth to the mid-nineteenth century*, UNESCO, Paris, 2003.

Bosworth, C E & Asimov M S (eds). *History of civilizations of Central Asia, Vol. 4, Part 2: The age of achievement: AD 750 to the end of the fifteenth century*, UNESCO, Paris, 2000 & Motil Barnasidass Publishers, Delhi, 2003.

Kalter, J. *The arts and crafts of Turkestan*, Thames and Hudson, London, 1984.

Kalter, J & Pavaloi, M (eds). *Uzbekistan: heirs to the Silk Road*, Thames and Hudson, London and New York, 1997.

Khakimov, A A, Akhmedov, A, Akilova, K, Kosakovskaya I, Alieva, S, Alieva, Z & Baratova, Sh. *Atlas of Central Asian artistic crafts and trades; Vol 1, Uzbekistan*, International Institute for Central Asian Studies, Samarkand, Sharq, Tashkent, 1999.

Razina, T, Cherkasova, N & Kantsedikas, A. 'Folk art in Central Asia and the Soviet Union', in *Folk art in the Soviet Union*, Aurora Art Publishers & Harry N Abrams, Leningrad & New York, 1989, pp358-458.

Sumner, C with Feltham, H. *Beyond the Silk Road: arts of Central Asia, from the Powerhouse Museum collection*, Powerhouse Publishing, Sydney, 1999.

Textiles, costume and accessories

Chepelevetskaya, G L. *Suzani Uzbekistana, Narodnaya dekorativnaya vyshivka*, Institut iskusstvoznaniya AN UzSSR, Tashkent, 1961.

Eiland, M L Jr (ed). *A world of oriental carpets and textiles*, International Conference on Oriental Carpets, Washington DC, 2003.

Franses, M. *The great embroideries of Bukhara*, Textile & Art Publications Limited, London, 2000.

Grube, E J. *Keshte, Central Asian embroideries: the Marshall and Marilyn R. Wolfe collection*, Marshall and Marilyn R Wolfe, New York, 2003.

Harvey, J. *Traditional textiles of Central Asia*, Thames and Hudson, London, 1997.

Kurbanov, B et al. *Applied art of Uzbekistan*, Ministry of Cultural Affairs of the Republic of Uzbekistan, Tashkent, 2003.

Pennell, S. 'The art of gold embroidery: a study of an aspect of traditional Uzbek material culture in transition', unpublished thesis, James Cook University, Townsville, 2000.

Sodikova, N. *National Uzbek clothes*, State Committee of Science and Technique of the Republic of Uzbekistan, Tashkent, 2001.

Sukhareva, O A. 'The design of decorative embroidery of Samarkand and its connection with ethnic ideas and beliefs', in *Soviet Anthropology and Archaeology*, (translated from Russian), M E Sharpe, New York, 1983-84.

Sychova, N. *Traditional jewellery from Soviet Central Asia and Kazakhstan*, Sovetsky Khudozhnik Publishers, Moscow, 1984.

Vok, I & Taube, J. *Suzani, a textile art from Central Asia: the Vok collection*, Herold Verlagsauslieferung, Munich, 1994.

Ceramics

Baipakov, K M & Erzakovich L B. *Ceramics of medieval Otrar*, Oner, Almaty, 1989.

Barry, M, Michaud, R & Michaud, S. *Colour and symbolism in Islamic architecture: eight centuries of the tile-maker's art*, Thames and Hudson, London, 1996.

Carswell, J. *Blue and white: Chinese porcelain around the world*, Art Media Resources, Chicago, 2000.

Dervis, G. *Sovremmenaia Keramika Narodnikh Masterov Srednei Azii* (Modern ceramics of national masters of Central Asia), Isdatelstvo Sovetskii Khudoshnik, Moscow, 1974 (in Russian).

Golombek, L, Mason R B & Bailey, G A. *Tamerlane's tableware: a new approach to Chinoiserie ceramics of fifteenth and sixteenth century Iran*, Mazda Publishers in association with the Royal Ontario Museum, Costa Mesa and Toronto, 1996.

Gray, B. 'Blue-and-white vessels in Persian miniatures of the fourteenth and fifteenth centuries', *Transactions of the Oriental Ceramic Society*, 24, 1948-1949.

Grube, E J et al. *Cobalt and lustre: the Nasser D Khalili collection of Islamic art. A survey of the arts of the Islamic lands*, Vol. 9, The Nour Foundation, London, 1995.

Peshereva, E M. *Goncharnoe Proizvodstvo Sredneii Azii* (Pottery production of Central Asia), Moscow & Leningrad, 1959 (in Russian).

Terres Secrètes de Samarcande: ceramiques du VIIe au XIIIe siècle, Institut du Monde Arabe, Paris 1992.

Watson, O. *Ceramics from Islamic lands*, Thames and Hudson, London, 2004.

Wilkinson, C K. *Nishapur: pottery of the early Islamic period*, Metropolitan Museum of Art, New York, 1973.

Wilkinson, C K. 'The glazed pottery of Nishapur and Samarkand', *Bulletin of the Metropolitan Museum of Art*, NS, Vol 20, 1961.

Zhalova, L A. *Sovremennaia Keramika Uzbekistana* (Modern Uzbekistan Ceramics), Moscow, 1963 (in Russian).

Acknowledgments

MANY PEOPLE CONTRIBUTED TO this publication and major exhibition.

Our special thanks are directed to the directors and staff of the participating museums in Central Asia. In UZBEKISTAN: Bukhara State Art and Architectural Museum, Robert Almeev (Director), Koryogdi Jumaev, Noila Kazijanova, Makhsuma Niyazova; Samarkand State Museum of History and Architecture, Nomon Mahmudov (Director), Rahim Kayumov, Lutfiya Marsipova; Tashkent State Museum of Applied Arts, Dr Turgan Dosteev (Director), Yulduz Yarmukhamedova, Karmil Tursunalaev, Tatiana Fomina; Tashkent State Museum of Temurid History, Professor Nozim Khabibullaev (Director). In KARAKALPAKSTAN (Nukus): IV Savitsky State Museum of Art, Marinika Babanazarova (Director), Aigul Pirnazarova. In TAJIKISTAN (Dushanbe): A Donish Institute of History, Archaeology and Ethnography, Academy of Sciences, Professor Rakhim Masov; Museum of Ethnography, Saodat Marufova (Director), Nadezhda Vasitova; National Museum of Antiquities, Dr Saidmurod Bobomullaev (Director). In KAZAKHSTAN (Almaty): A Kasteev State Museum of Arts, Baitursyn Umorbekov (Director), Amir Jadaibayev, Rashid Kukazhev; A K Margulan Institute of Archaeology, Academy of Sciences, Dr Roza Bekturieva (Director), Professor Karl Baipakov; Central State Museum, Dr Nursan Alimbay (Director), Gaisha Bakirova.

We are grateful to the President of the Republic of Uzbekistan, Mr Islam A Karimov; the President of the Republic of Tajikistan, Mr Imomali S Rakhmonov; and the President of the Republic of Kazakhstan, Mr Nursultan A Nazarbayev.

We also thank the following government representatives for their support: Republic of Uzbekistan — Mr Alisher Azizhodjaev, Deputy Prime Minister; Mr Boltaboy Shadiev, Presidential Administration; Mr Bakhrom T Kurbanov, Minister of Cultural Affairs; Mr Erkin Ernazarov, First Deputy Minister of Cultural Affairs. Republic of Karakalpakstan — Mr Sultan Atabaev, Minister for Foreign Economic Relations. Republic of Tajikistan — Mr Rajabmad Amirovich Amirov, Minister of Culture, and the former Minister of Culture, Dr Karomatullo Olimov. Republic of Kazakhstan — Mr Dyuisen K Kaseniyov, Minister of Culture.

The Australian Embassy in Moscow and the Department of Foreign Affairs have provided essential diplomatic support. We thank H E Mr Leslie Rowe, Ambassador of Australia to Kazakhstan, Tajikistan, Uzbekistan and the Russian Federation; Bruce Jones (Moscow); Susan Rose Allen (Canberra).

UNESCO support solidly underpinned the project. We thank Barry Lane, Head, UNESCO, Tashkent and Noriko Aikawa, Chief of UNESCO's Intangible Cultural Heritage Section; Dinara Abdullaeva, Guzal Bakhrambaeva, Elena Chemulova (Tashkent); Jorge Sequeira and Anjum Haque (former and current Heads) of UNESCO Almaty and Bolatbek Amanbekov, Sergey Karpov and Yuri Peshkov.

Support and encouragement were similarly provided by the National Commissions for UNESCO in Uzbekistan, Tajikistan and Turkmenistan. In Uzbekistan: Alisher Ikramov (Secretary-General); in Tajikistan: Dr Guljakhon Bobosadikova, Dr Lola Dodkhudoeva, Dr Munzifa Babadjanova (successive Secretaries-General), Suhrob Mirzoaliev; in Turkmenistan: Dr K Poladov (Secretary-General). We also thank the Oltin Meros Foundation in Uzbekistan.

In Central Asia, master (usto) craftswomen and craftsmen generously shared their knowledge and expertise: Akbar and Alisher Rakhimov (Tashkent), Nazrullo Abdullaev (Kitab), Mirzabakhrom Abduvakhobov (Andijon), Nomon Ablokulov (Urgut), Sulton Atadjanov (Kattabag), Ziyomiddin Davronov (Kasan), Azim Hotamov (Shakhrisabz), Eshonkulov Izzatullo (Boysun), Ibrahim Kamilov (Rishtan, who passed away two years ago), Zarina Kenjaeva (Bukhara), Mukhabat Kuchkorova (Shafirkhan), Rajabbiy Kholova (Urgut), Nomon Markhamov (Urgut), Abdullo Narzullaev (Gizduvan), Gulnora Odilova (Shakhrisabz), Rajab Ortiqov (Khiva), Farkhad Ramazonov (Shafirkhan), Rombergenov Saparbai (Chimbai), Bakhtiyor Sattorov (Kasbi) Safarboi Sokibov (Chorku), Kubaro Tokhtaeva (Urgut) and Muhammad Rasul Zukhorov (Denau).

For making their academic and institutional resources available, we thank in UZBEKISTAN: Professor Muzaffar Kamilov (Tashkent Institute of Oriental Studies), Dr Abdusobir Raimkulov, Dr Djamaliddin Mirzaahmedov (Samarkand Institute of Archaeology); in KARAKALPAKSTAN (Nukus): Professor Vadim Yagodin (Institute of History, Archaeology and Ethnography); in Kazakhstan: Dr Olga Kuznetsova (A K Margulan Institute of Archaeology), Dr Kenen Shikasil Akashuli (National Presidential Centre, Astana); in TAJIKISTAN (Dushanbe): Dr Nargis Khojaeva, Dr Alexander Kulyomin (A Donish Institute of History, Archaeology and Ethnography, Academy of Sciences), Dr Alla Aslitdinova (Central Scientific Library); in TURKMENISTAN (Ashgabat): Dr Mukhammed Mamedov (Monuments Protection and Restoration Department), Dr Ovezmukhamed Mametnourov (National Museum of Turkmenistan); in AUSTRALASIA: Ross Mitchell-Anyon and Suzanne Pennell.

For their integral role in realising this publication and exhibition we thank the Uzbek staff of Heritage Central Asia (Tashkent): Donyolbek Boltabaev, Ulugbek Ganiev, Svetlana Osipova, Nargisa Saidmaksumova and Rovshan Yuldushev.

Research was enhanced in many ways by contributions from David Best, Vera Chursina, Len Cook, Dee Court, Erica Froggart, Feruza Irgasheva, Sayora Irgasheva, Farhad Irgashev, Paul Jones, Sarah Kenderdine, Ross Langlands, Zarina Mulladjanova, Chester Nealie,

Jan Irvine-Nealie, Owen Rye, Brigid and Alan Waddams. Special thanks are also due to many Powerhouse Museum staff and volunteers, in particular Michael Desmond (Manager, Collection Development and Research), Claire Roberts (senior curator, International Decorative Arts and Design) Lindie Ward (assistant curator), and Rachel Miller, Heleanor Feltham and Olga Sawyer (Powerhouse Partners) for their indispensable individual contributions.

We also extend our grateful thanks to the Oriental Rug Society of NSW and the Gordon Darling Foundation for supporting Christina Sumner's travel to Central Asia in 2002 and 2003.

At last but not least, none of this would have been possible without the support of the Powerhouse Museum Director, Dr Kevin Fewster, and Deputy Director, Jennifer Sanders who championed this ground-breaking project.

Supporting authors

KORYOGDI JURAYEVICH JUMAEV is director of the Bukhara Art Museum and teaches theory and history of art in the Bukhara State University. He graduated from the Tashkent Theatre and Art Institute with the title of Art Expert and from 1975 to 2001 was director of the Bukhara Museum of Applied Arts, located in Sitorai Mohi Khosa, the Summer Palace of the last Amir of Bukhara. Mr Jumaev has curated a range of exhibitions and published widely on the applied arts of Bukhara. He is currently working on his PhD thesis on the embroidery of Uzbekistan in the 19th–20th centuries.

AKBAR RAKHIMOV is a distinguished Uzbek artist potter, whose father was an acclaimed ceramicist. He is a graduate of Uzbekistan's National Institute of Art and Design and an authority on the nation's traditional crafts. He is a full member of the Academy of Arts of Uzbekistan, and has received special honours from UNESCO for his work. He has recently established a national ceramics study centre in Tashkent with UNESCO and Uzbek government support. His works are represented in national and international collections. In recent years Akbar Rakhimov has led the technical investigations and revitalisation of traditional alkaline glaze technologies at the core of the UNESCO Blue of Samarkand Project.

ALISHER RAKHIMOV is Akbar Rakhimov's son and is now developing his own reputation as a nationally and internationally respected artist potter working in the family tradition in Tashkent. He also has travelled widely internationally as a lecturer, exhibitor and artist-in-residence.

Researchers

Compiling the information for this book would not have been possible without the knowledge and generosity of the senior curators, scientific researchers and other technical specialists from the lending institutions.

Lending institutions
UZBEKISTAN
State Museum of Applied Arts, Tashkent, Uzbekistan
State Museum of Temurid History, Tashkent, Uzbekistan
Bukhara State Art and Architectural Museum, Uzbekistan
Samarkand State Museum of History and Architecture, Uzbekistan
IV Savitsky State Museum of Art of the Republic of Karakalpakstan, Nukus

TAJIKISTAN
Museum of Ethnography, Dushanbe, A Donish Institute of History, Archaeology and Ethnography of the Academy of Sciences of the Republic of Tajikistan
National Museum of Antiquities, Dushanbe

KAZAKHSTAN
The A Kasteev State Museum of Arts, Almaty, Kazakhstan
The Central State Museum of the Republic of Kazakhstan, Almaty
The A K Margulan Institute of Archaeology, Academy of Sciences, Almaty, Kazakhstan

About the Powerhouse Museum

THE POWERHOUSE MUSEUM in Sydney is Australia's largest museum and is funded by the state government of New South Wales. Part of the Museum of Applied Arts and Sciences established in 1880, the Powerhouse Museum was purpose-built in 1988 in and around a disused power station. Its collection spans decorative arts, design, science, technology and social history, which encompasses Australian and international, and historical and contemporary material culture. The Powerhouse Museum has a reputation for excellence in collecting, preserving and presenting aspects of world cultures for present and future generations.

In 1997, the museum opened its Asian Gallery with the aim of promoting a greater awareness and appreciation of Asian cultures in Australia. Exhibtions in the gallery have included *Evolution & revolution: Chinese dress 1700s—1990s* (1997); *Rapt in colour:Korean costumes and textiles from the Choson dynasty* (1998); *Beyond the Silk Road: arts of Central Asia* (1999); *Earth, spirit, fire: Korean masterpeices of the Choson dynasty* (2000); *Trade winds: arts of Southeast Asia* (2001); and *Fruits: Tokyo street style* (2002).

Index